C000182817

GREAT Y

THE ROWS
and the Old Town

Colin Tooke

First Published 2000
by
Tookes Books
14 Hurrell Road
Caister-on-Sea
Great Yarmouth NR30 5XG

To Jan

Other titles in this series:
The Past Fifty Years
Front Line Towns
Caister 2000 Years a Village

No part of this work may be reproduced or stored in an information retrieval system without the express permission of the Publisher given in writing.

© Colin Tooke 2000

ISBN 0 9532953 3 8

Printed in England by Blackwell John Buckle
Charles Street, Great Yarmouth, Norfolk

Contents

A typical Yarmouth Row, partly paved and with overhanging houses, many of which date from the late 17th century. The entrance to another Row can be seen across the narrow north-south road in which the man is standing.

Introduction

The street plan of medieval Yarmouth consisted of three main streets aligned north-south connected by narrow east-west passage ways which from the late 13th century were given the name 'Rows'. Before 1813 it was impossible to cross the town from east to west without passing through one of these passage ways unless using Friars Lane at the extreme south end of the town or Fullers Hill at the north. The Rows, up to 156 of them with a total length of 7½ miles, were the heart of the old town and within them were to be found the homes of the majority of the townsfolk, from the wealthy merchants and ship owners to the more humble fishermen and their families. The three main streets of the old town were Charlotte Street (now Howard Street North) which continued southwards as Blind Howard Street (now Howard Street South), George Street and Middlegate (now Tolhouse Street). On the east side of the town was King Street and the Deneside while to the west was the river frontage, the Quays. These roads were all linked together in an east-west direction by the Rows. In 1848 there were 145½ Rows of which 134½ were passable for horses and 11 for foot passengers only.

In 1813 Regent Street was constructed to link the two main trading areas of the town, the Market Place and the Quayside. The Rows were preserved remarkably well until the Second World War when they were badly damaged by air raids. In the post war period large areas in the centre of the town were redeveloped and the Rows and most of medieval Yarmouth disappeared. It was during this period of rebuilding that new east-west roads such as Nottingham Way, Yarmouth Way, The Conge, Stonecutters Way and St Francis Way were created.

For five hundred years the Rows formed a unique system of 'streets' not found in any other town in this country. Recent research has compared them with similar early street patterns found in some Scandinavian towns, possibly reflecting the towns 11th century trading links.

The following pages look at the origins of the Rows, the names and later numbering scheme and a numerical list with the location of the Row, the various names and a brief description. Other chapters look at the north-south streets of the old town and what remains of the Rows today. The book is completed with an index of Row names.

The illustrations cover photographs of the Rows, the north-south streets and some of the buildings to be found at the corners of the Rows, including many public houses from which the Rows took their sometimes unusual names.

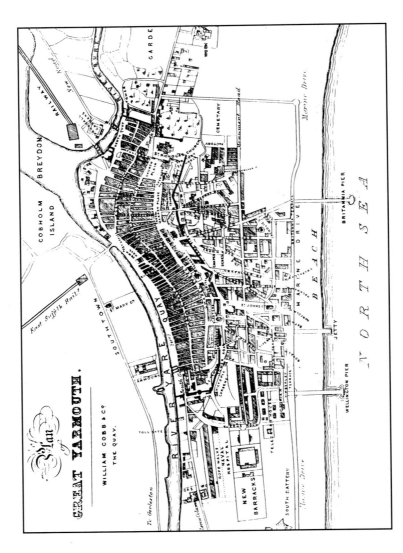

This map of 1860 shows the old town surrounded by the medieval wall and the new part of the town spreading towards the sea and the recently built Marine Drive. In the densely populated area of the old town the buildings are separated only by the three north-south streets and the 145 narrow Rows.

The Origins of the Rows

The medieval street pattern of Great Yarmouth, known locally as 'The Rows' has been a subject which has intrigued historians for many years. Nineteenth century writers put forward many differing theories as to the origin of these lanes, alleys or passages as they were sometimes called. All the early theories concerning the origin of the Rows have been dismissed by recent research. The basic layout of the town was possibly determined by a moving river line, the north-south streets following this line westwards. The curvature of the Rows, coupled with the fact that very few were aligned across the north-south streets could indicate that the early town builders followed the lie of the land rather than a predetermined plan. Land on the sandbank when it was first inhabited, c1000AD, was divided into basic units, long and narrow and aligned east-west. Early documents refer to these land units as 'rengiates' and as the population increased the rengiates became divided and subdivided until many buildings occupied the original strip of land. The space between the rengiates became the only access to many of these additional properties and these rights of way or 'common ways' were, from c1280, documented as 'Rows'. The width of these Rows varied considerably as did the space between them, sometimes only one house or building separating two Rows, sometimes two or more and occasionally two buildings back to back. In many cases there were small courtyards inaccessible except through the houses.

The town grew steadily from the 11th century and reached an economic peak between the years 1209 and 1336, mainly through the fishing industry. The highest part of the sandbank was in the Fullers Hill area and this appears to be where the first settlement was made. Archaeological excavation in this area in the 1970's revealed 11th century occupation layers and also confirmed the occupation areas to be in strips separated by narrow lanes or Rows. The same period for occupation of land further south was found in 1999 when excavations were carried out in the area of Rows 55 and 57, indicating the rapid spread of the town in a southerly direction. The town continued to expand until the latter part of the 13th century by which time it had reached its ultimate size. The southern limits of the town were determined by the buildings of the Blackfriars who acquired land to built a church and monastery there in 1271. The sea and the river determined the east and west boundaries. The northern boundary was determined by Grubbs Haven or Cockle Water, a shallow outlet of the river Bure to the sea between the town and Caister, although the early buildings did not extend this far north.

In 1261 King Henry III gave the townspeople a license to build a wall around the town, a project that was to begin in 1284 and take over one hundred years to complete. One reason for this lengthy building period was the Black

Death, the disaster which swept through the country in 1348/49 killing at least a third of the population. In Yarmouth it was recorded that 7050 people perished, no doubt the close proximity of the houses in the Rows helping to spread the disease. When the wall was eventually completed at the end of the 14th century it enclosed the town on three sides, the river giving the required protection on the western side. The wall enclosed an area which included the already established Rows. Only at the northern end of the town were houses forcibly pulled down to make their inhabitants move inside the new walled area

For the next four hundred years the town was to be restricted to its original size, unable to expand in any direction. The fortunes of the town rose and fell throughout the medieval period, the problems with the harbour entrance repeatedly silting up being one of the main reasons for economic decline. Following the completion of the seventh harbour entrance the period from 1650 to 1750 became one of renewed prosperity. Almost the whole town was rebuilt as an influx of Dutch settlers and a revival of the herring industry led to an increased demand for housing, and areas of the Rows which had lain waste since the Black Death were redeveloped. Large houses owned by merchants, ship owners and burgesses of the town were constructed, many of these being set back with a private court leading from the Row. For the majority of inhabitants however, the houses built at this time in the Rows were small with one room on the ground floor, one on the first floor and one room in the attic.

Rainbow Corner looking towards the Cross Row which led to Row 2. This was a very congested part of the town with many small houses. The Post Office and Fullers Hill car park are now on the site of Rainbow Corner and Square.

A basement was accessible only from the outside. The front door of these small houses opened into a passage which led through the house to a back doorway, one side of the passage being the dividing wall with the next house and the other side a wooden partition. A door in the partition gave access to the ground floor room, with a fireplace on the opposite wall. On one side of the fireplace was a cupboard, on the other side a winding staircase leading to the first floor room and the attic. The windows were small with diamond pattern lights, the attic room having no window. In houses of this design lived the majority of the inhabitants of the town.

In the following two centuries many of these small houses were enlarged by building extra rooms at the rear and the larger merchants houses were sub-divided into several tenements, with small dwellings built in the front court. This greatly increased the population density of a relatively small area and by the end of the 19th century many of the Rows had become overcrowded and unhealthy. Charles Dickens had penned an idyllic picture of the Rows in the middle of the century but in reality the situation for the inhabitants was far from satisfactory. An inquiry held in 1849, when the population was just over 26,000, into the sanitary conditions existing in the town reported that in many houses whole families were living in one room in overcrowded conditions where cholera, smallpox and other diseases were common. In Row 23 four cottages housed 24 people using one 'privy' which was only six feet from the sitting room door. The town had no piped water supply at this time and many of the 1500 wells within the walls were contaminated, several houses sharing one pump. In many cases the pump was against the wall of a privy cesspool or between two privies. Many houses relied on rain water cisterns to provide drinking water. There was no drainage system and all refuse went into cesspools several of which were to be found under bedrooms. The 'privies' were rarely emptied and often overflowed into the courts and Rows.

"In Row 78 is a small court 5 yards by 6 yards where two people have died with cholera. There is no drainage and no fresh air. The houses have no back doors or windows and the water supply is quite saline," said the report. The worst part of the town was the Fullers Hill area closely followed by Friars Lane. Even on the Denes, where new buildings were being erected between the walls and the seaside, there were 400 wells and no drainage system had been provided. Waste from the Victoria Hotel (now the Carlton Hotel) was allowed to form large pools on nearby ground.

There were many lodging houses in the old town – "the resort of rogues and vagabonds who prey upon society during the day and at night congregate in dens of immorality, filth and disease". In one such lodging house in Wrestlers Row, inspected in 1848, there were 20 persons in bed in two bedrooms.

By 1855 a Waterworks had been built at Ormesby and fresh water was being piped into the town via a reservoir at Caister. In 1875 a Sanitary Authority was created and this, together with the paving and lighting schemes, greatly improved the conditions in the Rows. Much substandard housing still existed, impossible to improve without large scale clearance and rebuilding, but for the people who lived there a strong community spirit existed within the close confines of the Rows.

A survey of the Rows undertaken in 1936 concluded that there were at that time considerable areas where general clearance was desirable to improve living standards, many houses unfit for habitation due to overcrowding and lack of light and air. A vast number of the houses could be improved by clearing away outbuildings and general reconditioning. Clearance started in some Rows but the outbreak of war in 1939 halted the work. The heavy bombing raids, particularly in 1941, damaged or destroyed large areas of the old town and in the early 1950's the remaining buildings were demolished to clear the central area of the town in preparation for rebuilding. Many people were reluctant to leave the area and a way of life which was to disappear for ever. What remained of medieval Yarmouth was now swept away and replaced by new housing and roads. Many people in the town today can still look back and recall their early lives in what Charles Dickens had called a 'gridiron' of streets.

A cobbled Row in the 19th century showing the 17th century housing which still existed at that time. It was these crowded conditions which led to the clearance orders of the 1930's. The lack of light and air in the overcrowded houses meant poor living conditions for many people.

Row Names and Numbers

The exact number of Rows has always been variable. As the town developed new Rows were constructed and others were taken into adjacent property. As early as the 13th century documents show that both the Greyfriars and the Whitefriars were allowed to take in Rows to enlarge their property. At the end of the 17th century new Rows appeared as buildings were constructed on the Deneside, open land between the town wall and what is now the western side of King Street. In 1813 two Rows disappeared when Regent Street was constructed and in 1890 several Rows were taken into Lacons Brewery as it expanded. In more recent times two Rows were taken into the new Woolworths store in the Market Place and Palmers Row was taken into the shop as it enlarged. The extension of the Conge and other new roads accounted for the loss of more Rows. The total at any one time probably never exceeded 156, a figure recorded in a survey of 1784 when there were 2500 houses and 12,608 inhabitants according to figures given by Dr Cooper, the Minister. By 1804 this number had dropped to 145 when they were officially numbered, although the numbering scheme did not include some half Rows and the already well known Market Row and Broad Row.

The numbers, allocated from north to south, replaced the many names by which the Rows were known at that time, names which at first reflected the trade or name of an occupant and later often the name of a public house associated with the Row. These names had changed with time until eventually a very confusing situation had arisen with any one Row having a variety of names. This can be seen in the following chapter where all the known names for each Row are listed, nearly six hundred in total.

The picture on the right shows George Street looking towards Fullers Hill in 1934.

Row 1, in the 19th century showing the 'hovels' as they were described by the Council. These were cleared away by January 1878. The 'red' herring which was part of the staple diet of Yarmouth people was often referred to as the 'Ramp Row Goose', a reflection of the poor quality of life which existed in this particular Row.

Part of Northgate Street usually referred to as White Horse Plain c1910. On the left is the tailors and costumier shop of Doughty & Baker and in the centre of the picture is the entrance to Fullers Passage which led through into Fullers Hill. The White Horse Inn is the white building and on the extreme right is the shop of George Chase, corn merchant.

The Rows: Past and Present

In the following list of Rows the number is that which was allocated in the 1804 numbering scheme and the number which can be seen on what remains of the Row today. Where the number is followed by * this indicates that some part of that Row still exists. The names are taken from many sources but it cannot be a definitive list because of the long period during which the Rows were known by name only, many of which were not documented. The location, given in italics, is the original location given here in a west to east direction. The description is as long as space in a book of this size permits.

Row 1
Rampart - Ramp
Common Ramp
North Quay to Northgate Street

The longest of all the Rows (300 yards) the name was taken from the rampart or town wall which ran along the north side and against which houses were built. The houses "of a very mean description" were demolished in the 1860's when they were described as 'hovels'. This section of the town wall, which led from the North Gate (demolished in 1807) was taken down in 1902 when Rampart Road was built. Today the site of the Row is the southern pavement of Rampart Road. At the SE corner was a public house called the Plough which was later renamed the Jolly Farmers and closed in 1867. A granary and later a malthouse stood on this corner site and more recently it was the Shortis Motorists Centre before laying derelict for many years. The buildings have recently been demolished.

Row 2 *
Black Horse - Bird in Hand
East and West Flegg
North Quay to Northgate Street

This Row was divided into two by a narrow cross row which ran from the town wall to Row 3. At the NE corner was the Bird in Hand, later the Black Horse and finally the East & West Flegg public house which closed in 1925. On the SE corner was the Huntsman & Horn

Row 3 *
Boulter's - Boulter the Baker's
Doughty's
Laughing Image Corner to Northgate Street

The bakery was on the NE corner until 1865. In parts the Row measured nine feet across and on the SE corner was the Horse & Groom public house which closed in 1925, now the Norfolk Kitchen Diner.

Row 4 *
Thornton the Grocer's
Ecclestone the Grocer's - Rolling
the Baker's - Wiltshire Arms
Laughing Image Corner to
Northgate Street

The Wiltshire Arms was on the NE corner, later to become Rudrum's ham and bacon shop. On the opposite corner was Thomas Thorntons shop, later Rollings, still a bakers shop and retaining the Rollings original facia.

Row 5 *
Burman's - Chapman's
Split Gutter
Rainbow Square to Northgate Street

A large open gutter at one time ran down the centre of this Row. John Chapman was a boot and shoe maker at the SE corner and on the NE corner more recently was the well known confectionery shop of Sullivans.

Row 6 *
Wigg's - Browne's - Douglas
Rackham's - Body Snatchers
Snatchbody
Rainbow Square to Northgate Street

Miss Ann Wigg was a resident of the Row as were Browne and Rackham. The name Snatchbody comes from the early 19th century practice of the Resurrection men who removed newly buried bodies from the churchyard to be used by medical students and surgeons in London. A cottage in this Row was the base for such a group until their leader Vaughan was imprisoned in the Tolhouse in 1827.

Row 7 *
Golden Keys - White Horse
Rainbow Corner to Northgate Street

At the SE corner was the Golden Keys, a public house which is today the White Horse Inn.

Row 8
Yew Tree - Ferry Boat
Rainbow Corner to Northgate Street

Opposite the western end of the Row was a ferry across the river Bure, replaced by a suspension bridge in 1829. The ferryman lived in a house at the SW corner of the Row. In a house on the north side of the Row was the first Wesleyan chapel in the town, opened in 1783 by John Wesley. A small beer house known as the Yew Tree was on the SE corner, later known as the Fishermens & Shrimpers Arms. This closed in 1904.

Row 8$^1/_2$

This half row had no name and ran in a north-south direction joining Rows 7 and 8 and leading into Rainbow Corner. A row of six houses known as Browns Buildings were in this cross Row.

Row 9
Bessey's Half - Bessey's
North Quay to Fullers Hill

A short steep Row leading from the top of Fullers Hill down to the Quay. The Bessey family lived at the SW corner, a house which later became the North Star, a public house popular with the Broadland wherrymen, many of whom lived in this part of the town. The Sawyers Arms public house was at the eastern end of the Row. This burnt down in 1841 and was replaced by the Albion Tavern which faced down the hill to Northgate Street.

Row 10
Horn - North - Brown the Candlemaker's - Tooley's Freeman and May's
George Street to Church Plain

Probably one of the oldest Rows. It was in this part of the town, on the highest part of the sandbank, the first permanent settlement was started by a small group of fishermen soon after 1000AD. On the south side of the Row was a chandlery where tallow candles were made from 1760 until the early 1800's by Brown and later Freeman and Mays. At the SE corner facing Church Plain was the shop of Tooley, a flour miller, later Wright's the bakers. In the 1960's this was Folkes the antique dealers. On the opposite corner was the furniture depository of Brett & Sons until demolished in the 1960's.

Row 11
Whitler the Baker's
North Garden
North Quay to George Street

Gardens which later became the site of St Andrew's church and school adjoined this Row. In the early 20th century a large salt water reservoir stood here, the water used to flush the streets and Rows. At the NE corner was a tavern known as the Royal Commissioners, a name later changed to the Brewery Tap, a Lacons house which closed in 1927.

Row 12
George and Dragon
George Street to Church Plain

The George & Dragon, a Lacons house, was on Church Plain on the corner of the Row. The site of this is now part of Falcon Court.

Row 13
Garden - South Garden
Lacon's
North Quay to George Street

This Row ran on the south side of the gardens described in Row 11. The western end opened into Besseys Piece, open land where touring circuses at one time performed. Lacons owned maltings at the SW corner of the Row and by 1895 the south side was taken up by the buildings of Lacon's Brewery.

Row 14
Goymer's Meeting North
Baptist's Meeting - Brett's
North - Rev. Green's Meeting
George Street to Church Plain

The religious names are taken from the meeting house or Baptist Chapel in Row 15 which had a rear entrance into this Row. As in Row 13 the south side was taken up by the buildings of Lacon's Brewery.

Row 15
Goymer's Meeting South
Jeffery's - Brett's South
Rev. Green's Meeting
George Street to Church Plain

The chapel stood on the north side of the Row from 1756 until 1871. In 1890 this Row was absorbed into the Brewery, the chapel becoming part of the bottling store. At the NE corner was the shop of Robert Ceiley a herbalist and medical botanist, famous for his worm pills and powders. Ceiley later moved, still on Church Plain, to near the church gates, a shop which is today a hairdressers.

Row 16
Lacon's - Lacon's Brewery
George Street to Church Plain

Almost opposite this Row in George Street stood the Grapes Tavern, another victim of the Brewery expansion in 1890.

Row 17
Says Corner North
North Quay to George Street

Says Corner was a name given to an opening off North Quay, a name taken from a family once owning property there. Dr. Thomas Girdlestone lived at the NW corner of Says Corner from 1792 until 1822, a doctor of some distinction seen daily in the town always dressed in black with silk stockings, half gaiters, white cravat, frill shirt, powdered wig with pigtail and carrying a gold headed cane. This Row was another taken into the Brewery in 1890.

Row 18
Says Corner South
Says Corner to George Street

Another Row absorbed by Lacons Brewery in their 1890 expansion.

Row 19
Wrestlers - Brewery
Lacon's Office
George Street to Howard Street

The Wrestlers public house on Church Plain was opposite the entrance to this Row. This corner of Church Plain led into Howard Street, earlier called Charlotte Street The last mail coach driver in the town, Tom Colman, lived in this Row. In 1927 the eastern end of the Row was bricked up as by this time it led into the Brewery premises.

Taken in 1971 this aerial view of the Fullers Hill area shows the demolition of the property in Laughing Image Corner, Rainbow Corner and Rainbow Square in preparation for the construction of the new bridge and road layout. The maltings in Rampart Road were later demolished when the Telephone Exchange was built.

Laughing Image Corner. The white building stands between Row 1 and the Corner and was at one time the Lord Collingwood public house. The roadway seen here now runs between the Telephone Exchange and the Post Office Sorting Office.

August 1971 and the new road under construction to the east of the North West Tower.
In the background are the buildings of Lacons Brewery, soon to be demolished.
To the right of the Tower is the bridge across the river which was replaced in
1972 by the present bridge linking with the A47 road.

In 1972 these maltings in Rampart Road were demolished to make way for a new
Telephone Exchange at Laughing Image Corner. This view is the south side of the
maltings with the White Swan public house on the left of the picture.

The wall plaque records that this house stood on the site of the cottages which became the first Wesleyan Chapel, opened 22 October 1783 by John Wesley. The site is now the Fullers Hill car park.

Between Rows 10 and 12 stood a shop and the George and Dragon public house which gave its name to Row 12. Throughout the war years this became the wine and spirit order office for Lacons following the bombing in 1943 of Burroughs on the corner of Church Plain and the Market Place, now the site of the Gallon Pot. The George and Dragon originally belonged to the Yarmouth brewery of Pagets which was on North Quay. This brewery was demolished in 1847 when the railway bridge was constructed.

Row 20 *
Wrestlers Tap - Bailiff Barett's
Swan - Two Necked Swan
Stewards Chemist
Howard Street to Market Place

Robert Barett was bailiff in 1488. The Two Necked Swan (a name taken from the custom of 'nicking' the bills of swans on the river Thames to denote ownership) is still at the SE corner, previously known as The Three Flowers de Luces (a Norfolk corruption of fleur-de-lis). This public house was also known as Smedley's for many years, after Bert Smedley the landlord until 1952. On the opposite corner was another public house, the White Bear. Until the 1980's this property was the chemist shop of Steward & Sons, today a restaurant.

Row 21 *
Fill the Auctioneer's
Smith the Cabinet Maker's
George Street to Howard Street

James Fill lived at the SE corner and the Smith family, cabinet makers, upholsterers and paper hangers later occupied the same property. On the north side of the Row was a passage linking to Row 19 and here were Kemp's cow sheds. Cows were kept in several Rows, taken out to graze on the marshes each day. Lacon's offices were erected at the NE corner in1885. The north side of the Row formed the boundary of the Brewery site and now runs beside the Tesco store.

Row 22
Shuckforth Basket Maker's
Feltham's - Bumpstead's
Barnes the Grocer's
Howard Street to Market Place

Bumpstead's grocery shop, later Barnes, was at the NE corner, today Claxton's clothes shop. This is now the north pavement of the Conge.

Row 23
Tooke the Baker's - Baxfield's
Fromow the Barber's
Traynier's Fish House
George Street to Howard Street

The Fish Houses of Henry Traynier, demolished c1880, stood on the north side of the Row. Fromow was a barber whose shop was on the NE corner.

Row 24
Blue Anchor - Pickard's
Foulsham's
Howard Street to Market Place

Lamp Passage ran from the south side of this Row. The Blue Anchor public house was at the SE corner next door to Foulsham's Hotel and Restaurant. The restaurant closed in 1947. The Blue Anchor closed in 1964 and was demolished, rebuilt as the Westminster Bank. This Row is now the south pavement of the Conge. At the SW corner was the Ropemakers Arms.

Row 25
Fighting Cock - Cobb's
Doughty the Leather Cutter's
Doughty's North
Coach & Horses - Golden Lion
George Street to Howard Street

At the NW corner was the Fighting Cock, a name later changed to the Coach & Horses and then the Golden Lion, finally closing in 1929. At the SW corner were extensive maltings which extended through to Row 27 in the 19th century.

Row 26
Taylor the Surgeon's
Dr Smith's - Half Moon Tap
Half Moon North - Bee Hive
Lorimer the Grocer's - Wild the
Baker's - Penny's - Norman's
Howard Street to Market Place

A small beer house called the Bee Hive, later the Fishermans Arms was at the NW corner. On the opposite corner was the Griffin, renamed the Keel then the Duke of York and finally the Victoria, a notorious public house favoured by foreign seamen. The basement was known as Hell's Hole. The Victoria lost its license in 1880. Lorimer the grocer was in business in 1863 and in 1822 Dr James Pearson Smith resided here. At the NE corner was Norman's the cabinet makers, still trading as a furniture business today although the Row has been blocked.

Row 27
Well - Doughty's South
Doughty the Leather Cutter's
Cobb the Currier's South
George Street to Howard Street

The premises of Cobb and Doughty extended from Row 25 to this Row. The name Well Row comes from a deep well in a yard midway along the Row, used by people from a wide area. Other tradesmen living in this Row were 'Old Smith' a watercress seller, Folkes the basket maker, Gibbs the twine spinner and Jones the bird-fancier.

Row 28
Conge
North Quay to George Street

Originally the Conge was a narrow street running from the Quay to George Street. This unusual name first appears in documents dated 1286 and could be derived from the nearby bend in the river Bure. Henry I appointed a Provost or collector of duties who resided here and the adjacent Quay was called the Lords Quay or Kings Conge. As a street name it is probably unique in this country. The Conge was linked to Row 28 by Angel Passage. At the SW corner was the Falcon public house previously known as the Excursion Train Tavern. This closed in 1940 and was demolished, part of the site later becoming Self's Garage, now an office block.

Row 29 *
Half Moon - Half Moon South
Kings Head North - Edinburgh
Queens Head North
Davy the Watchmaker's
Howard Street to Market Place

At the Market Place end of the Row the Kings Head was on the south corner and the Half Moon on the opposite corner. This latter public house became the Edinburgh and closed in 1922. The Kings Head was from 1971 until 1989 known as the Growler and now the Market Tavern. At the other end of the Row was the Queens Head which closed in 1940. The Police Station now stands on the site of the Queens Head.

Row 30
Barnaby the Baker's
Wheel of Fortune
George Street to Howard Street.

The Wheel of Fortune was on the NW corner. It closed in 1938 when the license was transferred to the new Links Hotel at Gorleston.

Row 31 *
Nine Parish
North Quay to George Street

This Row originally formed the northern boundary of the White Friars whose monastic buildings were destroyed by fire in 1509. Five houses still stand in this Row with a passage leading through to Row 34.

Row 32 *
Kings Head - Kings Head South
Queens Head South
Howard Street to Market Place

The Market Tavern in the Market Place occupies the site between Row 29 and this Row as did the Queens Head at the Howard Street end. A house in this Row was the home of Josiah Curtis, town crier or bellman for 32 years.

Row 33
Dr Farmington's
Nightingale the Barber's
George Street to Howard Street

Dr Farmington lived in this Row early in the 18th century.

Row 34 *
Quay Mill
North Quay to George Street

A windmill, known as the Quay Mill, stood near the river opposite the end of this Row from c1580 until 1799. On the north side of the Row were the Cherry Tree Tea Gardens. A row of houses known as Cherry Tree Cottages still stand on this site today. At the NW corner was a public house known as the Quay Mill which closed in 1942. It was earlier known as the Windmill, Hunter Cutter and the Railway Hotel or Tavern. This is now the site of Kingdom Hall.

Row 34¹/₂ *
Quay Mill Alley - Eagle Half
From North Quay

On the corner of this short Row was the Eagle Tavern, a Steward & Patteson house which closed in 1907.

Row 35
Harman's - Rowe's
Freemasons Arms - Globe
Howard Street to Market Place

The Globe was on the SW corner, a disreputable beer house which was closed down in 1861. John Rowe was a bailiff in 1622 and lived at the SE corner.

Row 36
Neal the Shoemaker's
Mouse the Pawnbroker's
Ames the Shoemaker's - Garden
George Street to Howard Street

Six houses on the north side of this Row had small front gardens, an unusual feature in the Rows. In 1857 Arthur Patterson the naturalist was born at No 8. Many tradesmen lived in this Row in the 19th century, several of their trades having disappeared today. Among them were a shoemaker, rope and twine spinner, bill poster, hairdresser, whitesmith, tailor, painter and glazier as well as a master mariner and a customs officer.

Row 37 *
Glass House - Absolon's
North Quay to George Street

In the mid 18th century there was a glass factory on the north side of the Row, in Glasshouse Passage, run by William Absolon. At the NE corner was Lombard House, a building which from 1825 was used as a Roman Catholic chapel and schoolroom until the new church was built in Regent Road in 1850. Lombard House then became Phillips the pawnbrokers.

Row 38 *
Ferrier's - Charles Moore's
Ellis the Brushmaker's
Howard Street to Market Place.

The Ferrier family lived at the SE corner, Richard Ferrier being bailiff in 1691. In the 19th century this house became the shop of Freeman the leather worker. Stephen Ellis was a brushmaker who lived and worked in this Row.

Row 39
Norman the Cabinet Maker's
Blowers the Cabinet Maker's
George Street to Howard Street

Mark Blowers, upholsterer and cabinet maker lived here until 1871. Simon Norman of the same trade moved from here to the Market Place early in the 20th century (see Row 26).

Row 24 can be seen to the right of Foulsham's Dining Rooms and the Blue Anchor public house, seen here in 1899. Five years earlier Lacons had taken over the Blue Anchor and they later purchased the Dining Rooms. In 1947 the Dining Rooms closed and the whole building became the Blue Anchor which was to continue until 1964 when it was demolished and a new branch of the Westminster Bank built on the site, opening in 1966.

The Kings Head public house was in 1822 known as the King Georges Head, today it is the Market Tavern. In the 18th century cock fights took place here and in the days of the stage coach the Telegraph Post Coach left here daily at 5pm for Norwich and the Accommodation Coach left at 10am for Bury every Sunday, Tuesday and Thursday.

This wartime picture of the shops on the west side of the Market Place shows the boarded up shops of William Patrick, Outfitter at number 16 and next door Southey's Bazaar, between Rows 26 and 29.

These cottages were in Row 29, Half Moon Row, and are typical of the many 17th century dwellings to be found in the Rows. The Half Moon at the Market Place corner of the Row was famed for its Skittle Alley and Concert Room. In the 1850's the violinist and acrobat Charles Marsh often performed here. In May 1863 Marsh fell to his death from the Nelson Monument on the South Denes while attempting to climb out onto the figure of Britannia to play his violin.

Howard Street North looking north. On the right are Taylor's Refreshment Rooms, Row 36 and the Queen's Head Public House, now the site of the Police Station.

George Street looking across the top of the Conge in 1934. It was not until after the War that the Conge was continued through to the Market Place. George Street was one of the original narrow medieval north-south streets in the town, running from Fullers Hill to Hall Quay. In 1886 there were thirteen Public Houses in this street as well as many small shops and houses. In 1890 a lot of property at the northern end of the Street was demolished when Lacons expanded the brewery site.

Row 40
Wall the Linen Draper's
Fulcher the Grocer's
Taylor and Fulcher's North
Howard Street to Market Place

In the Market Place between this Row and Row 43 was the Central Cinema which opened in 1915. This was renamed the Plaza in 1928 and from 1942 was used by Marks & Spencer as a temporary shop. The cinema building was demolished in 1958 and a new store for Woolworth's built on the site, Rows 40 and 43 being taken into the new building.

Row 41
Rose and Crown
King the Baker's
George Street to Howard Street

The Rose & Crown was a Lacons public house at the NE corner which closed in 1923, the property later becoming the dairy of Frank Gooda.

Row 42
Barnby the Liquor Merchant's
Jews - Synagogue
Hunt the Glazier's
George Street to Howard Street

For many years a Jewish Synagogue stood in this Row, the last one being opened in 1847. By the end of the 19th century the Jewish congregation had diminished to a point where it was no longer viable to hold services and the synagogue was closed.

Row 43
Dassett's - Hogarth's
Taylor and Fulcher's South
Moon the Cabinet Maker's
Howard Street to Market Place

Described in the 19th century as a narrow and gloomy Row having lofty houses on each side. John Dassett was a prominent figure in the town early in the reign of Charles I. Between this and Row 44 was a public house called the Colchester, later the Edward VII. In the 1930's it was renamed the Burton Arms, rebuilt in 1959.

Row 44 *
Angel - Markland's
Howard Street to Market Place

The Angel Inn in the Market Place was one of the oldest inns in the town, dating from at least 1652. It closed in 1939 and throughout the war was the British Restaurant. The building was demolished in 1957 and shops built on the site. At the SW corner in Howard Street was the City of London Tavern, formerly the Green Man and Boot. The site was rebuilt in the 1950's as the Talbot. In the Row itself were two beer houses, the Cross Keys belonging to Lacons and the Nags Head owned by Paget's brewery. Francis Markland was a chemist and druggist with a shop at the NE corner of the Row, later Carpenters the tobacconist and now the Heart Foundation charity shop.

Row 45
Woolsey's School - Singens
St John's Head
North Quay to George Street

This Row formed the southern boundary of the White Friars (see Row 31). Leading off the north side was Troy Alley. From 1801 until 1868 clay tobacco pipes were manufactured in this Row and at the NW corner was the town mortuary. The line of this Row is now the south pavement of St Francis Way.

Row 46 *
Sewell's - Sewell the Grocer's
Nags Head
Howard Street to Market Place

Sewell's grocers shop was at the NE corner, property which later became Back's public house which closed in 1981 and was rebuilt with a gift shop at the front and a public house, Back to Backs, in the Row.

Row 47 *
White Swan - Golden Ball
Pipemaker's
Page the Pipemaker's
North Quay to George Street

Thomas Page the pipemaker had a workshop in this Row later taken over by James Taylor, also a pipemaker, until 1889. At the NW corner is the St Johns Head which in 1787 was called the St John Ale House.

Row 48 *
Bartholomew's - Wheat Sheaf
William the Fourth
North Quay to George Street

The Wheat Sheaf was a public house at the SE corner, renamed the Mitre Stores. In recent years it has been known as Fagins, Speakers (1994), Phoenix (1996) and now again the Mitre. John Bartholomew was bailiff in 1582.

Broad Row *
Old Broad - Kingston House
George Street to Howard Street

A Row not included in the 1804 numbering scheme this was known as Broad Row on account of its width. When a new Broad Row was created further south, later to become Queen Street, this Row became known as Old Broad Row. In the 13th century it was known as Kingston House Row. Many large merchants houses were to be found in this Row and from the mid 18th century this was one of the few Rows where shops appeared. These included cordwainers (shoemakers), drapers, hairdressers and a brazier. Boots the Chemist opened a shop here in 1896 and the family firm of Plattens began in 1889. Other traders included William Absolon and James Taylor (see Row 47). Robert Ellis a brushmaker traded here until 1932. A passage off the north side of the Row was known as Newark's Passage, after a blacksmith of that name in 1826.

Market Row *
Howard Street to Market Place

Until the early 19th century this was a busy thoroughfare for carts from Broad Row to the Market Place. In 1820 it was "stopped up for the convenience of foot passengers" and soon became a popular shopping area. By 1836 there were 42 different traders established in this Row including Abraham Cooper the ironmonger. The firm of John Woodger, herring curers, had a shop here. They claimed to be the first to kipper herring, in 1846. In 1897 they cured over 20,000,000 kippers for the London market. An early Lacons beer house, the Turkey Cock, was in this Row in 1796.

Row 49 *
Blake the Linen Draper's - Vine
Howard Street to Market Place

The Vine public house was at the Howard Street end of the Row. Known for a short time as the Howard Distillery the house closed in 1934.

Row 50
Symonds the Hairdresser's
Lane the Taylor's
Richmond the Cabinet Maker's
George Street to Howard Street

At the NE corner was the New Queens Head, a public house closed in 1926. The Row is now the north pavement of Stonecutters Way.

Row 51 *
Lamb - Black Swan
Howard Street to Market Place

The Lamb, later called the Black Swan was at the SW corner. This closed in 1910 and was later used by Hunts Mineral Waters to produce their new line of 'County Toffee'. On the south side of the Row was Canister House (see page 34).

Row 51$^{1}/_{2}$
Half - British Lion Alley
From Market Place

This short Row led from the Market Place and turned north into Row 51. At the corner was the British Lion, earlier known as the Plow. In the 1960's this was the Market Place site of the coffee shop of Purdys, known as the Kenya Coffee Bar.

Row 52
Buck - Costerton the Surgeon's
Dr. Costerton's - Bunting's
Hall Quay to Howard Street

Dr Costerton was Mayor in 1825. The Buck was on the SW corner and closed in 1927. It was demolished in 1930 when a new toilet block was built on the site. On the south side of the Row was Owle's Court, after Owle the chemist whose shop was on the Quay and backed onto the court. This Row now forms the south pavement of Stonecutters Way.

Row 53 *
Turners Bank North
Bank Paved
Hall Quay to Howard Street

On the SW corner is the bank of Barclays which was erected in 1854 as the bank of Gurney & Co. On the opposite corner is the Bank of Scotland which in the 1920's was the London Joint City and Midland Bank. Until 1871 this was the site of the Post Office and before that a Gentleman's Club. On the NE corner was the Exchange Vaults public house, named after the neighbouring Corn Exchange.

Row 54
Smith the Baker's - Almshouse
Palmers Arcade
Howard Street to Market Place

The Almshouses in the Row were sold in 1842. Until the 1970's the Row divided the shop of Palmers Ltd. and was referred to as Palmers Arcade until absorbed into the shop.

Row 55 *
Turners Bank South
Gurneys Bank - Meggy's - Skill's
Meall's - Cobbs the Printer's
Barbers Stationer's - Clowe's
Hall Quay to Howard Street

At the SW corner was a book shop owned successively by Downes, Meggy, Skill, Barber, Meall and Cobb. From 1870 the shop on the NW corner was Clowes the grocers which closed in 1940. After the war this became the temporary home for the town library until the new one was built behind the Tolhouse.

Row 56
Excise Office - Savings Bank
Howard Street to Market Place

The Excise Office was at the NW corner, later becoming the Savings Bank until this moved to the Market Place. At the SE corner was the Elephant & Castle public house, later named the Market Distillery and then the Red House, a house famous for the model railway in the bar. This closed in 1961 and was rebuilt as Downes supermarket, now Mackays, the Row being taken into the building.

Row 57 *
Carpenters Arms
Mr Brightwen's - Star &
Garter - Sarah Martin's
Hall Quay to Howard Street

The original Star & Garter was on the SW corner, earlier called the Crown & Thistle. This moved to the opposite corner when Lloyds bank was extended. The Carpenters Arms at the SE corner changed its name to the Great Eastern Hotel in 1866, Silver Herring in 1969 and then in rapid succession Oakwood, McCourts, Ringside, Legends, Burnt Oak, Morgans and today Caspar Jacks.

Broad Row looking towards George Street in 1923 when Stead & Simpson
had a shoe shop on both sides of the Row.

This ornate lamp standard was a feature of Broad Row in the 1880's.
This view of the Row is looking towards Howard Street.

Bradleys the outfitters shop on the corner of Broad Row c1936. Until 1934 this had been one of the shoe shops of Stead & Simpson (see page 27). This shop became Norfolk Radio until 1960 and was then demolished, the site now an open space on the corner of Broad Row and Howard Street.

The first Marks & Spencer shop in the town in George Street c1926.
This was opposite Broad Row, now the site of a car park. Marks & Spencer remained here until moving to King Street in 1932.

The Market Row shop of Sayers. By the 1920's this was Stead & Simpson shoe shop and later Bevington's the chemist. Today it is a tea room.

The outfitters R & T Martin traded in Market Row for over one hundred years before their recent closure.

Other well known traders in the Row in the 1970's included Court's Furnishers, Fielding's Cycle Shop, Hannant's Toy and Model Shop, Cooper's Tool Shop, Olivettes Wool Shop, Pike's Tobacconist, Bevington's the Chemist, Fisher's Photographic Studio and on the Market Place corner Vettese's Restaurant.

ECONOMY AND FASHION !

R. & T. MARTINS,

Tailors, Hatters, Hosiers & Outfitters,

MARKET ROW, YARMOUTH.

Selected New Materials of the Best Manufacture

FOR

SUITS, COATS, TROUSERS & VESTS.

∴ Silk and Felt Hats. ∴

FLANNEL TENNIS and BOATING SHIRTS.

FORD'S "EUREKA" SHIRTS.

FOOTBALL HOSE, SWEATERS, AND JERSEYS.

GENTLEMEN'S UNDERCLOTHING in ፨ ፨
SANITARY WOOL, MERINO, COTTON, etc.

Waterproof Garments of Guaranteed Make.

GENTLEMEN'S ALPACA AND SILK UMBRELLAS. ∴ SCARVES, TIES, AND GLOVES IN GREAT VARIETY.

Row 58
Elephant & Castle
Last the Baker's - Red House
Howard Street to Market Place

In the Market Place the Elephant & Castle extended from Row 56 to this Row. In the 19th century a basket maker, a chair maker and a costermonger lived in the Row.

Row 59 *
Woolhouse's - Crown & Anchor
Upcher's - Mitchell's School
Hall Quay to Howard Street

Ralph Woolhouse was bailiff in 1558, 1567, 1579 and 1590 and lived at the NW corner of the Row. The Upcher family lived in the house for many years before moving to Sheringham Hall. The house was then used as a school by the Misses Susan and Hariet Mitchell and in 1821 the Elizabethan building became a bank which by 1918 had become Lloyds. A fireplace dating from 1598 can still be seen in the building.

Row 60 *
Oxford - Deneside Austin
Ostend Market - Randall's
Bassingthwaite the Baker's
Howard Street to King Street

This Row led to the site of the Augustine Friars, part of which was bought in 1694 by the Quakers who erected the present Meeting House in 1807 at the western end of the Row.

Row 61 *
Popinjay - Coalmeter's
Quay Austin - Ostend West
Hall Quay to Howard Street

The Coalmeters public house was on the Quay at the NW corner. This was later called the Earl St Vincent and then the Steam Packet which was demolished in 1939 and the Yare Hotel built on the site of this and the adjacent Crown & Anchor. On the south side of the Row, towards the western end, was a beer house known as the Rope Dancers and later the Blue Anchor, demolished in 1808. Samuel Palmer, mayor of the town three times, later built a house on this site which in the late 19th century was rebuilt as the National Provincial Bank. The Mariners Tavern, originally known as the Three Jolly Mariners, stands at the Howard Street end of the Row.

Row 62 *
Church's - Symond's
Homfray's - Ben Dowson's
Hall Quay to Howard Street

The Star Hotel now stands at the NW corner, a building which until 1930 was the Cromwell Temperance Hotel. The original Star was on the opposite corner until demolished to build a Telephone Exchange in 1934. Benjamin Dowson was a maltster and corn merchant who lived at the SW corner of the Row.

Row 63 *
Post Office - Old Post Office
Bond the Druggist's - Sloman's
Nall's - Quakers
Howard Street to King Street

Until 1840 the Post Office was in this Row. At the SE corner was the shop of Charles Sloman bookseller and printer, later the business of George Nall. Today it is still a book shop, that of Jarrold & Sons.

Row 63¹/₂
Post Office Half
Tomlinson's - Turnpike
From Howard Street

This half Row from Howard Street turned north into Row 63. The Yare Hotel was on the NW corner, a building which in 1909 became the town's Telephone Exchange.

Row 64 *
Mew's - Bateman's
Pritchard's
James Burton's Half
King Street to Theatre Plain

Until the middle of the 16th century land south of the Market Place was open land known as the Deneside. In 1678 Mitchel Mew, bailiff in 1681, was the first to build a house on this land, creating a new Row. John Prichard was a surgeon living at the NW corner, later the home of Dr Stafford. Today Marks & Spencer's store is between this and Row 65.

Row 65 *
Cups - Mariners
Jay's Chemists
Dakin the Brazier's
King Street to Theatre Plain

Dakin the brazier was at the SW corner of this Row. The Cups, now the Theatre Tavern is on the SE corner in Theatre Plain which takes its name from the Theatre Royal, opened in 1778 and demolished in 1928.

Row 66
Girling's - Dendy's
Stamp Office - Savings Bank
Howard Street to King Street

Edmund Girling was an amateur artist of some merit, born in this Row. Crown Court led off this Row and here the first Saving Bank was established in 1818. When Arnolds new store was rebuilt following the disastrous fire of 1919 this Row was taken into the new building, later Debenhams department store.

Row 67
Nicholas Cutting's
Mayor Ramey's - Star Tavern
Hall Quay to Howard Street

Nicholas Cutting was bailiff in 1619. At the SW corner was The Black Boys, rebuilt in 1747 as the home of John Ramey, mayor in 1760. The original Star Tavern was at the NW corner (see Row 62).

Row 68
Thomas Lucas's - Bream's
Hall Quay to Howard Street

Thomas Lucas was bailiff in 1658. At the SW corner was the house of Samuel Bream, later a lodging house where Sir Richard Onslow and Admiral Lord Duncan stayed. In 1813 this Row was taken into the new Regent Street.

Row 69
Rev. Welham's - Hurry's
Howard Street to King Street

John Welham was minister of St George's and headmaster of the Grammar School. His house in the Row was later owned by George Hurry. This Row was also taken into Regent Street in 1813.

Row 70 *
Foreman the Baker's
Craske the Baker's
Male the Chemist's
Howard Street to King Street

Male the chemist was at the King Street end of the Row and on the opposite corner was the Crown. This became a public house in 1834 and was demolished in 1967, two shops being built on the site one of which was Dewhurst the butchers, now a bakery. Today this Row runs at the rear of the property facing Regent Street.

Row 71 *
Symond's - Cubitt the Painter's
Hall Plain to Howard Street

Nathaniel Symonds, a merchant, lived at the NW corner and Robert Cubitt a plumber and glazier lived at the SW corner. On the SW corner was the Hall Tavern or Town Hall Tavern, opposite the side entrance to the Town Hall. This public house closed in 1890 and is now The Kitchen.

Row 72 *
Haynes the Peruke Maker's
Moore the Blacksmith's
Hall Plain to Howard Street

At the NW corner lived William Haynes a peruke (wig) maker. The property was later that of Samuel Moore, an anchor smith and in 1900 it was a restaurant. By the 1930's this was the office of the Yarmouth Mercury. On the opposite corner was Camplings the printers which later became the Yare Printing Company.

Row 73
Barker's North - Cobb's North
Boatswains Call
Miller the Basket Maker's
Howard Street to King Street

The Boatswains Call was a public house on the corner of this Row. At the King Street end was a Lyons restaurant in the early 20th century. There was a large malthouse in this Row, towards the western end.

Row 74
Barker's South - Cobb's South
Fasset's - Peacock's - Aldred's
Howard Street to King Street

At the NE corner lived Samuel Barker, mayor in 1800. It was at this house Admiral Lord Nelson was entertained when he visited the town in 1800 after his victory at the Battle of the Nile. Samuel Cobb, mayor in 1837, later lived at the same house. This Row disappeared when the Central Arcade (now the Victoria Arcade) was constructed in 1926.

Row 75 *
Poppy's - Spilling's
Old Fountain North
Middlegate Street to Howard Street

Jonathan Poppy was a large man who lived at the SW corner. His trade was that of an auctioneer but in times of trouble he was sworn in as a special constable. This Row ran from the point where Hall Plain became Middlegate Street.

Row 76 *
Peer's - Samuel Tolver's
Cory's
South Quay to Middlegate Street

John Peers owned land to the south and was bailiff several times in the late 15th century. Samuel Tolver, mayor in 1789, lived at the NW corner. The Police Station was at the NE corner in the 1880's.

Row 77 *
Coach & Horses - Old Fountain
Old Fountain Tap
Norfolk Tavern
Three Feathers
Middlegate Street to Howard Street

On the SW corner was the Three Feathers public house, later the Coach & Horses, closed in 1805. On the opposite corner was the Fountain, later the Norfolk Tavern, the Middlegate Distillery and, since the 1930's, Allens. At the Howard Street end there was a malthouse on either side of the Row.

Row 78 *
Pot in Hand North
Pot in Hand - Cambridge
Bett's - Starling the Hatter's
Brown the Grocer's
Howard Street to King Street

The Pot in Hand was a public house on the King Street corner which in 1834, was described as "a common resort of men and women of low character". The name changed to the Champion and later rebuilt as the Cambridge which closed in 1911. For many years this was the shop of Smiths, dyers and cleaners. On the opposite corner was the shop of John Starling a hatter, which by the 1920's had become the Maypole Dairy. These properties were all rebuilt in the late 1950's following war damage but the Row entrance was retained.

Canister House Row 51. This drawing by the Norwich artist Noel Spencer is one of a series which appeared in the Yarmouth Mercury under the title, "Corners of Old Yarmouth". The artist captured many scenes in the Row area of the town just before they were demolished in the 50's and 60's. Canister House was an imposing 18th century house and was at one time the home of John Harris, a clay tobacco pipe manufacturer. These pipes were made in enormous quantities in the 19th century; a pipe kiln would fire 80,000 at one time and the pipes sold for 2/6 ($12^{1}/_{2}$p) per gross. John Harris was the last pipe maker in the town and died in 1932.

The Market Distillery, later known as the Red House at 40 Market Place. On the right can be seen Row 54 (Palmers Arcade) and under the sign 'Saloon Bars' is the entrance to Row 58. In the 1920's the property to the south of the public house became Palmers men's department, 41 & 42 Market Place. In 1961 the Red House closed and for a while this was Palmers men's department but in the 1970's the site was redeveloped as a new supermarket for Downs, later Fine Fare. Palmer's department store expanded at the same time and took Row 54 into the shop.

In Howard Street South was the Exchange Vaults public house, on the corner of Row 53. This building was part of the adjacent Corn Exchange, a building used for many types of public entertainment as well as its intended commercial use. When it was owned by Mr Foulsham of the Dukes Head, 500 diners could be accommodated in the Corn Exchange, the fascia stone of which can be seen today outside the library in Tolhouse Street. Other names for this public house were the Corn Exchange Vaults and the Exchange Stores.

FOR BREAKFAST,
FOR SUPPER,

THE MOST DELICIOUS, REFRESHING
AND SUSTAINING DRINK,

Is a CUP OF HOT COCOA,
MADE FROM

CLOWES'

PURE

Cocoa Essence

per **1/8** lb.

More economical than the widely advertised Cocoas.

ONLY TO BE OBTAINED AT

CLOWES' STORES,

THE PURE FOOD SPECIALISTS,

Hall Quay, Great Yarmouth,

And Branches.

Clowes Stores at 15 and 16 Hall Quay, on the corner of Row 55. Founded in 1758 this was one of the high class grocers in the town, the two shops also selling all kinds of household requirements from stationery to wicker baskets. The shop closed in 1940 and after the Second World War the building became the temporary town library following the destruction of the old building in Row 108. It remained the library until the new building at the rear of the Tolhouse opened in May 1961. Part of the building seen here was taken over by Aldreds & Partners in 1966.

The large house in Row 57 (right), was known as Nelson House, through its association with Lady Hamilton who was said to have stayed here. Another resident of this Row was Sarah Martin the prison reform worker who hired a room in a house here while she worked as a seamstress and visited the inmates of the Tolhouse gaol.

Row 79
Pot in Hand South
Jolly Maltsters - Lobster
Three Pigeons
Howard Street to King Street

At the SW corner, in Howard Street, was the Three Pigeons public house which later became the Lobster, the Jolly Maltsters and by 1874 the Enterprise. This closed in 1952. In the 1930's the Yare Printing Company occupied premises along the north side of the Row. For many years the shop of Tom Green, hatter and hosier was at the SE corner in King Street.

Row 80
Hardware's - Harmer's
Worship's North
Worship the Attorney's North
Miss Patterson's
Harbord the Pastrycook's
Lone the Pawnbroker's
Howard Street to King Street

George Hardware, bailiff in 1612 and Robert Harnmer, bailiff in 1652 lived in a large Elizabethan house in King Street between this and Row 82. Later residents of the house were the Worship family in the 19th century. A large malthouse occupied the central part of this Row through to Row 82. Harbord's pastry shop in King Street later became Hill's Restaurant, rebuilt after the bombing of the Second World War as Matthes Restaurant, today a fitness centre. This Row and Rows 79 and 82 were lost.

Row 81 *
Crome's - John Berney's
Lettis's - Meyrick's
Rumble the China Dealer's
King Street to Deneside

John Berney Crome was the son of John Crome, founder of the Norwich School of Painter and lived at the NW corner. Dr Lettis was the parish surgeon and lived in the Row.

Row 82
Swindon the Historian's
Worship's South - Worship the Attorney's South
Baptist Meeting North
Howard Street to King Street

On the south side of the Row was a Baptist chapel known as the Bethabara Chapel. Henry Swindon, one of the town's foremost historians lived at the SW corner.

Row 83 *
Cooper's - Carter's
Charles Palmer's - J D Palmer's
Sayers the Attorney's
Aldred's
South Quay to Middlegate Street

Benjamin Cooper built a large house at the NW corner in 1596, later to become the home of John Carter, John Danby Palmer and the Aldred family. Today this merchants house is restored as the Elizabethan House Museum, No 4 South Quay.

Row 84 *
John Ireland's - Ship Tavern
Middlegate Street to Howard Street

The house of John Ireland at the SW corner later became the Ship Tavern. After the battle of Camperdown in 1797 officers who had been taken prisoner were detained here. The building on north side of the Row was the Sunday School of the Congregational Chapel, in recent years part of the Art College, destroyed by fire in 1999.

Row 85 *
Baptist Meeting South
Old Library - Sir Sidney Smith's
Arbon the Painter's - Marsh's
Crown and Heart
Howard Street to King Street

The first public library was founded in a building at the NE corner in 1802. This later became the pawnbrokers shop of Frederick Marsh until destroyed by bombing in 1941. The Crown & Heart was an old beer house in King Street which closed in 1834.

Row 86 *
Fisher's - Fielding's
J C Smith's
King Street to Deneside.

John Fisher, an 18th century merchant lived at the NW corner, a house later belonging to Benjamin Fielding a surgeon. On the SW corner was the house of Drs Wyllys, Wyllys and Ley.

Row 87 *
Steward's - Money Office
George the Fourth
Howard Street to King Street

On the King Street corner today is Peggotty's public house. This was originally the Sawyers Arms then the George IV. By 1850 it was St Georges Tavern and then St Georges Wine Vaults until 1975.

Row 87$1/2$

This unnamed Row ran between Rows 87 and 89. There were nine houses in this short cross Row.

Row 88
Ames the Antiquary's - Creed's
Woodward's
Fowler the Grocer's
Middlegate Street to Howard Street

Joseph Ames lived in this Row in 1730, later selling his house to William Creed.

Row 89 *
Old Hannah's Back - Herring's
Hans Herring's
Howard Street to King Street

This was a very narrow Row, John Herring a ham curer living at the NE corner. At the NW corner in Howard Street was the William Tell Tavern.

Row 90 *
Old Hannah's - Mew's Half
Bellamy's - Harrison's
Balls & Pownall Fruiterer's
Middlegate Street to King Street

Howard Street South, formerly known as Blind Middlegate, ended midway along the south side of this Row. Mitchell Mew was bailiff in 1670 and Balls the Fruiterer was at the King Street end. In this Row lived John Hannah who was accused of murdering his wife in 1813. After being found guilty he became the last person to be publically hanged on the North Denes.

Row 91 *
King Street to Deneside

This short Row did not have a name and there was no property in the Row itself. At the SW corner was the photographic studio of Alfred Price, later Frank Sayers, both well known photographers in the town. The Victorian facia of this shop has in recent years been uncovered and restored, 28 King Street.

Row 91¹/₂
Greyfriars - Cloister
From Middlegate Street

This short Row led to the remains of the medieval Greyfriars Cloisters where in the 19th century four cottages had been built in the ruins.

Row 92 *
Carrington's - Hurry's
Bethabara - Old Meeting House
Unitarian Chapel
South Quay to Middlegate Street

This Row was formed in 1657 through land which had originally been part of the Greyfriars. The Carrington and later Hurry families lived in a house at the SW corner. Between this and Row 96 in Middlegate Street was the Old Meeting or Unitarian Chapel, built in 1845. This was destroyed in 1941 and the present chapel built almost on the same site.

Row 93 *
King the Baker's
Rivett the Baker's - Kings Head
Goddard the Whitesmith's
Middlegate Street to King Street

The bakers shop was on the SW corner where for many years bread for the poor was baked, a 4lb 14oz loaf being sold for 3d (1p).

Row 94
Joseph Cotman's - Wood's
Penrice Back
King Street to Deneside

Joseph Cotman lived at the NW corner and was mayor in 1745, 1757 and 1759. Later Captain William Larke RN, first governor of the Naval Hospital on the South Denes lived in part of this house. Alexander Woods was a solicitor who lived in the Row.

Row 95 *
Kittywitches
Draper the Butcher's
Middlegate Street to King Street

Probably the best known of all the Row names this was a picturesque but gloomy Row with many overhanging Tudor houses on the south side. At the King Street end the Row was four and a half feet wide but narrowed to only 30 inches at the western end. In the 17th century a baker by the name of Christopher (Kit) Witchingham lived in the Row and soon Kit Witchingham became abbreviated to Kittywitches. There have been many theories over the years as to the origins of the unusual name, including stories about witches and other strange happenings in this Row.

Row 96
Town Arms - Bush Tavern
Wildgres North - Turks Head
Old Meeting South - Fuller's South
Quay to Middlegate Street

John Fuller lived in a large house between this and Row 100 on South Quay. The Row is now partly the southern pavement of Yarmouth Way. At the NW corner was the Peace & Plenty public house, later the Bush. At the SE corner was a small beer house called the Town Arms, by 1740 known as the Dolphin and later the White Bear. In 1842 it was renamed the Turks Head and destroyed by bombing on 9 July 1941.

Row 97 *
Barnes - Blick's - Bell's
Bayly's Surgeon - Nightingale
the Confectioner's
Lawyer Bell's - Norfolk Hero
Middlegate Street to King Street

Joseph Bayly was a surgeon who lived at the SE corner and Samuel Bell was a solicitor who lived in the Row. On the SW corner in Middlegate Street was the Norfolk Hero beer house which closed in 1901.

Row 98
Urquahart's Back
King Street to Deneside

This Row was absorbed into the mansion built by Thomas Penrice which extended from St Georges Plain to Row 94. The house stood for only 40 years before being demolished and a Congregational Chapel was built on the site in 1855, now known as Christchurch.

Row 99 *
Castle
Middlegate Street to King Street

Until 1621 a castle stood in the vicinity of this Row although the exact position is unknown. At the NE corner was a public hose known as the King of Prussia, later the North Country House and finally the Old Jamaica Rum Stores. This Lacons house closed in 1931 and was then for many years Cubitt's fish shop.

Looking south along King Street c1908. The Music Shop of Arthur Watts is now the Age Concern Charity shop.

A tram on its way to the Wellington Pier via St Peters Road makes its way along King Street in August 1902 when the town was decorated for the Coronation of Edward VII. The shop with the striped blinds is Starlings the hatter and hosier at number 171 on the corner of Row 78.

Row 91¹/₂ leading from Middlegate Street to the medieval remains of the Greyfriars Cloisters. The buildings were severely damaged during the bombing of the town during the Second World War and when restored, the 18th and 19th century cottages that had been built within the ruins were removed. Today the site is looked after by English Heritage together with the other preserved Row properties, the Merchants House and the Row 111 houses.

The Greyfriars were one of several monastic orders that established themselves in the town in the 13th century. Their extensive lands between Rows 83 and 96 included a church (now the site of Queen Street) and monastic buildings of which todays ruins are only a small part. The cloisters connected the church with the domestic buildings. The Greyfriars were of the Franciscan order of friars recognised by their grey habits. Today the only surviving medieval wall painting in the town can be seen on a wall within these ruins.

Above - a house in Row 99, Castle Row, being demolished during the late 1930's clearance. In the 1920's there were thirty-one houses in this Row.

On the right is Row 95, Kittywitches Row. This picture is looking towards King Street, the widest end of the Row and the part which still survives today. The Middlegate end, the site of which is marked today by a small plaque on the wall of the flats, was barely thirty inches wide making it the narrowest of all the Rows. Many sinister traditions have been associated with this Row including claims that witches at one time lived here. All these are however fictional but it is a fact that in the 17th century the official witch-finder Matthew Hopkins visited the town and condemned 16 women as being 'in league with the devil' and thus had them executed. Kittywitches Row is probably the best known of all the named Rows and has featured on more postcards than any other Row.

Row 100 *
Spooner's - J F Costerton's
Sowell's - Sowell the Painter's
Fuller's South
Sons of Commerce
South Quay to Middlegate Street

John Fisher Costerton the town water bailiff lived in this Row. This was an important office responsible for collecting dues from shipping (see Row 106). William Spooner was bailiff in 1699 and mayor in 1713. At the South Quay corner was the Rampant Horse, renamed the New Custom House when the nearby house of John Andrews (see Row 103) was first used as the Custom House. This public house later changed its name to the Sons of Commerce.

Row 101 *
Reynold's - Charles Symonds
Victualling Office
Penrice Stable
Middlegate Street to King Street

Charles Symonds lived at the SE corner. The stables for Penrice House were in the Row, the site later becoming the Penrice Arms public house which changed its name to the 151 Club in 1978. In Middlegate Street between this and Row 102 lived Jacob Arnold a beer brewer. The business was sold in 1775 to Malletts brewery and in 1802 taken over by Reynolds who had just erected a new brewery on the Denes.

Row 102 *
William's - Benett the Cooper's
Arnold the Brewer's
William & Bells - Packet Office
Middlegate Street to King Street

The Packet Office was at the SW corner, an office for the packet-boat which plied between Yarmouth and Cruxhaven during the war with France. In 1795 all the mail for the Continent, except Spain and Portugal, left the Kingdom by this route through Yarmouth. On the opposite corner was the retail shop of Williams, Frere and Company wine and spirit merchants. This bow fronted building still exists. At the NE corner is the Brunswick Hotel.

Row 103 *
Royal Exchange - Andrew's
Saffrey the Brewer's - Chapel
Custom House
North Custom House
South Quay to Middlegate Street

John Andrews, said to have been the wealthiest herring merchant in Europe, built a house at the SW corner of this Row in the 18th century. In 1812 this was purchased by the Government and used as the Custom House. The Royal Exchange public house was at the NW corner, later becoming the Crane Hotel owned by Morgans brewery. This closed in 1962. The Suffolk Tavern was at the NE corner in Middlegate Street a public house which closed in 1950.

Row 104 *
Swanard's - Martin's
Robert Warmington's
Friendly Society - Dr Collier's
Custom House South
South Quay to Middlegate Street

The ancient name of Swanards originates from time when the keeper of the town's swans lived there. Mary Bennett, victim of the Yarmouth Beach murder, lodged in a house in this Row in 1900 under the name 'Mrs Hood'. Her husband was found guilty and hanged at Norwich Prison after a trial at the Old Bailey in 1901.

Row 105
Chapel - Rev. Cooper's
Dr Penrice's
Doughty the Grocer's
Middlegate Street to King Street

This Row led to the open space on Deneside where St Georges Chapel was built in 1714. The Rev Cooper and later George Penrice lived in a large house at the SE corner. Today the site of this Row is part of Yarmouth Way.

Row 106 *
Couldham's - Gaol North
Three Cranes - Dutch Chapel
Palgrave's - Town House
South Quay to Middlegate Street

At the NW corner was the Town House, erected in 1600. This building was also used as a Dutch Chapel, a library and one of the first theatres in the town. It was damaged in 1941 and later demolished, the site today being the road to the Central Library. At the SE corner stands the Tolhouse, today a museum but for many years the seat of civil government in the town and the Gaol. The Three Cranes public house was at the SW corner until 1775. In 1900 the building opened as the YMCA which it remained until 1934. Part of the building is now the Great Yarmouth Mercury office.

Row 107 *
Post House - Old Post House
Chapel Paved - Step Paved
St Georges East
Middlegate Street to King Street

The town's first Post Office was established here in the 17th century, known then as the Post House. This was the only Row not level with King Street, steps leading down into the Row. At the SW corner was a public house known as the Welcome Sailor, later the Tolhouse Tavern.

Row 108 *
England's - Anthony Taylor's
Walking - Gaol Paved
St Georges Paved West
Free Library - John Fisher's
South Quay to Middlegate Street

This was the first Row to be paved with flagstones. The Bird in Hand public house, later the Tuns Inn was to be found in the Row.

Row 109 *
Red Lion - Dr Borrett's
Dr Meadow's - Lion & Lamb
Middlegate Street to King Street

The Red Lion public house was at the SW corner, this closed in the 1890's. On the opposite corner was the house of Dr Borrett, later Dr Meadows. The Lion & Lamb at the SE corner was in the 1980's renamed Kitty Witches, now Liberty's Rock Cafe.

Row 110 *
New Prison - Prison
Perry the Oatmeal Maker's
Bellamy the Butcher's
Middlegate Street to King Street

Buildings on the south side of the Row were purchased by the government in 1803 and converted into a prison where French prisoners were detained during the war with France. Bellamy & Sons the butchers were on the SE corner in King Street.

Row 111 *
Luson's - Sir Eaton Traver's
Lucas's - Steward's
South Quay to Middlegate Street

The Lucas family and later the Stewards lived at the NW corner. On the SW corner was the house of William Luson later the home of Sir Eaton Travers. In 1858 this became the Yarmouth College. Three houses in this Row, numbers 6, 7 and 8 have been restored by English Heritage.

Row 112 *
Holmes South - Tomkins School
Brown the Maltster's
Chambers the Sailmaker's
South Quay to Middlegate Street

Leonard Holmes, bailiff in 1623, lived at the SE corner. The Yarmouth College, run by Daniel Tomkins, was between this and Row 111.

Row 113 *
Tilson's South - Errington's
Ferrier the Surgeon's
Middlegate Street to King Street

Thomas Tilson was a member of the Corporation in 1626. George Errington lived at the SE corner, a house which was later to belong to William Ferrier. In the Row, near the Middlegate end was a beer house known as the Bee whose sign read:

> Within this hive, we're all alive,
> Good liquor makes us funny;
> If you are dry, step in and try
> The flavour of our honey.

Row 114 *
Lieutenant White's
Willis's Half
King Street to Deneside

A large house to the north, fronting St Georges Plain, was the home of Sir Astley Cooper, an eminent 19th century London surgeon. On the SW corner was the Gas Showroom, now the Sea Change offices and gallery.

Row 115 *
Nathaniel Fish's - Batchelor's
King Street to Deneside

Nathaniel Fish lived in a house at the NW corner. This property was for many years the office of the Yarmouth Gas Company, now it is Kings Wine Bar.

Row 116 *
Sam Hurry's - Thomas Hurry's
Plummer's - Plummer's School
Hastings the Pawnbroker's
Middlegate Street to King Street

The Hurry family, ship owners and general merchants, lived at the SE corner. The house was later purchased by Joseph Plummer who established a large boarding school known as Jaynes Young Ladies College. In 1889 this became the drapers shop of Mr G Carr, taken over in 1908 by Skippings. This shop closed in December 1997.

Row 117 *
Josh Peartree's - The George
Ballast Keel - Matthew Ward's
Gallon Can
South Quay to Middlegate Street

Joshua Peartree lived in a house at the NW corner which later became the George and renamed the Greenland Whale Fishery. In 1795 it was known as the Ballast Keel and subsequently the Gallon Can which closed in 1999. The Merchants House, a restored 17th century property is in this Row.

Row 118 *
Blue Bell - White Swan
Hall the Blacksmith's
South Quay to Middlegate Street

The White Swan was on the NW corner, a public house which closed in 1950 and was demolished.

Row 119 *
Couldham's - Dawson's
Bradnack's - Dove
Robinson the Grocer's
Middlegate Street to King Street

Aleyn Couldham lived at the NW corner in 1534, later the home of Stephen Dawson. The well known botanist and antiquary, Dawson Turner was later born in this house. At the SW corner was the Harmless Dove, a public house which had a bad reputation and changed its name in 1822 to the Sailors Return. It was later changed to the London Tavern and closed in 1903.

Row 120 *
Duncan's Head - Drum
Humber Keel
Middlegate Street to King Street

The Duncans Head was at the NE corner, later named the Humber Keel or Humber Sloop. In 1835 Lacons bought the site, demolished the old building and opened the York. When this closed the name was transferred to the Imperial Hotel opposite, on the corner of York Road.

Three employees of Harry Moore the wine merchants whose address in 1900 was 177 King Street, the corner site which was later the Crown Hotel. At the top of the building, in the north east corner, was a round glass window with an inset crown lit at night. This photograph was taken in Row 70 at the rear of the premises.

A typical Row scene c1900. The surface of many Rows left much to be desired for the pedestrian, some were paved with beach pebbles (described by Charles Dickens as "petrified kidneys") and open gutters were common. Eventually a scheme to pave all the Rows got under way and paving slabs replaced the uneven surfaces. Gas lamps began to appear in many Rows in the 19th century although during the hours of darkness most Rows were still formidable places for strangers

Above is Middlegate Street
looking north c1900. The
Tolhouse is one of the town's
oldest buildings and the public
house on the opposite side of
the road, the building with the
man standing outside, was the
Tolhouse Tavern (right). This
public house on the corner of
Row 107, St Georges Row East,
had previously been known as
the Welcome Sailor, a name
intended to attract trade from
the nearby quay area. By 1895
the name had changed when it
was bought by Lacons brewery
for £1300. The public house
closed in June 1933.

People look out of their doors as an unknown photographer takes this picture of their Row in the early years of the 20th century. Note the small bird cages on the wall of the houses on the right, a common sight today in many Mediterranean countries.

Row 121 *

Huke's - Huke the Carpenter's
Captain Christmas's
Middlegate Street to King Street

At the Middlegate end of the Row was the grocers shop of Sam Rudrum and on the opposite corner Woolseys' Stores, a general clothing and furniture store. There were 21 houses in this mainly residential Row.

Row 122 *

Spread Eagle
Martin the Shoemaker's
Middlegate Street to King Street

The Spread Eagle public house was in King Street on the opposite side of the road, a popular 19th century house with a concert room. This closed in the 1890's and its popularity is reflected in the fact that a Row on the opposite side of the road carried its name.

Row 123

John Fisher's - Dover Colby's
North Wall - Quay Angel
Colby's North
Fulcher the Pawnbroker's
South Quay to Middlegate Street

John Fisher, mayor in 1767 lived in the Row. The Angel or Quay Angel was at the NW corner and Dover Colby lived in a house between this and Row 124.

Row 124

Cat & Monkey - Colby's South
Trotter Bar - Dover Colby's
South Wall
Laws and Lamb the Butcher's
South Quay to Middlegate Street

The Cat & Monkey beer house, later the Ship, was on the NW corner and demolished in 1754. On the opposite corner was the Colliers Arms owned by Morgans brewery and closed in 1924. At the SE corner was the Magdala Tavern which closed in 1941.

Row 125 *

Mack the Tinsmith's - Gun
Middlegate Street to King Street

This was one of the Rows where a gun barrel was placed at the corner to stop the troll carts damaging the buildings. Mack the locksmith and ironmonger had a shop at the King Street end. Between this Row and Row 127 in Middlegate Street was the Gallon Pot or Gallon Can earlier known as the Tumbledown Dick.

Row 126 *

Robins Half - Kemp's
Goods the Grocer's - Calver's
St Peters Half Alley
King Street to Deneside

John Robin, bailiff in 1678, built a large house on the north side of the Row. The close proximity to St Peters church gave it the name St Peters Half Alley.

Row 127
Scott the Baker's - Foundry
Yetts Foundry - Thompson's
Middlegate Street to King Street

Yetts Foundry was established in 1835 on the south side of the Row. In 1895 it was taken over by Walter Brett and continued working until destroyed by an air raid in 1941.

Row 128
Garwood the Glazier's
Woolverton's
Spanton's Factory - Bond
South Quay to Middlegate Street

Woolverton & Son, painters were at the South Quay end of the Row, the building later becoming a Labour Exchange.

Row 129
John Taylor's - Friends
Gregory Harrison's - Druids
Newcastle Tavern
St Peter's Paved West
South Quay to Middlegate Street

The Oddfellows public house was at the NE corner. On the SW corner was the Diana Packet later the Fishery and then the Newcastle Tavern. This later changed its name to the Ferry Hotel, a Lacons house which closed in 1941. In the Row on the south side was another public house, the Gun Tavern.

Row 130
St Peters - St Peters East
White Lion North
Old White Lion
Middlegate Street to King Street

The Old White Lion on the SE corner has been a tavern for at least 250 years, prior to that it was the house of a wealthy merchant James Symonds. The building still retains some of the 17th century features such as panelling and carved door heads. Between this and Row 127 in Middlegate Street was the Foundry Arms or Iron Founders Arms taking its name from the foundry in Row 127. There were at least eight shops in this Row, an unusual feature because shops were to be found in the north-south streets of the town except Market Row and Broad Row. Today the Row forms the southern pavement of Nottingham Way.

Row 131
Woolverton the Cooper's
Beckett's - White Lion South
Middlegate Street to King Street

The Rows in the southern part of the town were mainly inhabited by people connected with the fishing industry and in this Row lived three fish merchants and five fishermen in the 19th century.

Row 132

Present the Butcher's
Adam the Barber's
Cook Ellis's - Marsh's
Orfeur's - Dover Court - Delf's
South Quay to Middlegate Street

Garson H Blake lived in a large house at the South Quay end of the Row. At the NE corner was Delf & Sons wholesale confectioners, makers of sweets and rock.

Row 133

Trendle's - Union - Crisp the Carter's - Graves the Pieman's Spratt the Shoemaker's - Lee the Pawnbroker's - Bellamy the Baker's - John Cooper's North
South Quay to Middlegate Street

John Trendle was bailiff in 1624, the site of his house on the NW corner later became the Bell & Crown public house which closed in 1940. Like many of the public houses on corners of Rows there was a 'Jugs' entrance in the Row itself. John Cooper owned a grocers shop at the Middlegate Street end known as the People's Tea Mart.

Row 134

Echard's - Knights the Baker's New White Lion - Wake's
Middlegate Street to King Street

The New White Lion or Little White Lion at the King Street end of the Row closed in 1904.

Row 135

Hayes the Butcher's
Tomlinson Arms - Emm's
Butcher's - Old Prison
Middlegate Street to King Street

Thomas Emms lived at the NW corner, in a large house part of which was later to become the Tomlinson Arms beer house which closed in 1911. Matthew Butcher lived on the opposite corner.

Row 135$^1/_2$

Cock Half - Blanchflower's Half
From King Street

This short cul-de-sac ran to the rear of the Cock Tavern in Middlegate Street. On the corner of the Row, 95-97 King Street was Blanchflowers potted meat and game factory whose products were packed in china pots. About 1918 this factory was sold to the Co-op and became the Co-op Canning Factory, damaged by bombs in 1941 and then used as the town mortuary.

Row 136

Bracey's - John Cooper's South New Fountain - Almshouse Three Herrings
South Quay to Middlegate Street

Andrew Bracey, mayor in 1714, lived at the NW corner. At the SW corner was the Yarmouth Arms later the Three Herrings, a public house which finally became the Upper Ferry. The New Fountain was at the NE corner.

Row 137
Grief's - G D Palmer's
Rose & Crown - Horse & Cart
Cart & Horse
South Quay to Middlegate Street

G D Palmer was a surgeon who lived in the Row. The Rose & Crown and the Cart & Horse were two beer houses in the Row in the 18th century.

Row 138
Dog & Duck - Union
South Quay to Middlegate Street

The Dog & Duck was a small 19th century beer house at the NW corner.

Row 138$^1/_2$

This unnamed half Row ran in a north-south direction between Rows 137 and 138. The houses in this half Row were known as Durrants Cottages.

Row 139
Paget's - Mission to Seamen
Matthew the Baker's
South Quay to Middlegate Street

At the SW corner was the home of Samuel Paget, father of Sir James Paget, the eminent 19th century surgeon after whom the hospital at Gorleston is named. In 1863 this house became the Government School of Art and Navigation later changing to the Municipal School of Science.

Row 140
Liverpool Tavern
Earl St Vincent - Stevenson's
Ives the Antiquary's
Dene Well - Pigeon
Middlegate Street to King Street

John Ives, an 18th century antiquary and historian, lived in a house between this and Row 135. At the SE corner in King Street was the White Swan, a small public house later known as the Earl St Vincent which closed in 1940. At the SW corner was the Liverpool Tavern.

Row 141
Spotted Cow - Nelson Tavern
Houghton the Baker's
Child the Blacksmith's
Middlegate Street to King Street

The Spotted Cow at the SE corner was later known as the Nelson Tavern. Child the blacksmith lived at the Middlegate end of the Row.

Row 142
Felstead's - Thaxter's - Pigeon's
Kerrisons Coffee Tavern
Fishing Boat - Peacock
Mariners Compass
South Quay to Middlegate Street

Thomas Felstead lived at the SE corner. On the SW corner was the Mariners Compass later known as the Distillery. At the NE corner was the Peacock later called the Fishing Boat.

Row 143
Grosse's - Maye the Baker's
Woodroffe the Grocer's
Pleasant the Grocer's
Morling the Grocer's
South Quay to Middlegate Street

The grocers shop of Gabriel Woodroffe and later Daniel Morling was at the SW corner. This later became Durrants, grocer and ships bread baker and was demolished late in the 19th century and the Seamen's Mission Church and Institute built on the site.

Row 144
Jone's - Neave's
Thorndick's - Mayer's
Southgate the Butcher's
Middlegate Street to King Street

This was the last Row in King Street, most of the inhabitants being fishermen.

Row 145
Nag's Head - Hat & Feather
Fourteen Stars
Nottingham Arms
South Quay to Middlegate Street

At the SW corner was the Nags Head, renamed the Hat & Feather and then the Unicorn which closed in the 1890's. At the NE corner was the Fourteen Stars, later called the Nottingham Arms, closed c1889.

New Broad Row

This is today known as Queen Street. This area was part of the lands belonging to the Grey Friars and sold by the Corporation in 1657 to John Woodroffe on condition that he made a broad row and a narrow row (Row 92) for the convenience of the public from the Quay to Middlegate. On the SW corner was a large warehouse belonging to Thomas Hurry & Co., ship agents and iron merchants. Adjoining this in Queen Street was the Queens Head which later became known as the Golden Lion. On the SE corner with Middlegate was the Black Lion public house.

Priory Row *
Church Plain to Priory Plain

This Row formed the southern boundary of the Priory buildings which were originally the home of the Benedictine Monks connected with the Parish Church of St Nicholas. The large Georgian building on the NW corner was the vicarage, erected in 1718 and extended in 1786. On the opposite corner is a small house which for many years was the house of the Parish Clerk.

The picture on the left shows Nos. 74 to 76 Middlegate Street in 1906. To the right is the Cock Inn when Charles Neslen was landlord, this became the Middlegate Tavern in the 1920's and closed in 1940. On the left of the picture is the small shop of S Middleton which a few years later became Thomas Sparham's (see below). This was typical of the small bow fronted shops to be found in Middlegate. It was this shop which Charles Dickens used in his book David Copperfield as Mr Omer's the draper and undertaker who arranged Mrs Copperfield's funeral and the shop where Emily worked as a dressmaker.

The small shop of Thomas Sparham, 74 Middlegate Street in 1910.
A man of many trades.

On the corner of Row 117 was the Druids Arms in Middlegate Street. Edgar Aldous was landlord in the 20's and 30's and next door at number 151, on the corner of Row 112, lived Horace Butcher, a rag merchant. One day in 1934 Edgar found Horace lying on the floor of his shop, his head having been battered with a heavy iron weight. The Horace Butcher murder has remained one of the unsolved mysteries of the town. The Druids Arms was originally owned by the Colchester Brewery Co. and later became a Lacons house.

The Middlegate Tavern was earlier known as the Cock Inn, one of the oldest beer houses in the street. It was rebuilt in the 1870's. In 1927 Frank Sydney Clover was the landlord and between this and Row 140 was the Co-op Wholesale Society Fish Depot, part of which can be seen on the right. When the Middlegate Tavern closed in 1940 the spirit licence was transferred to the new Iron Duke at the north end of the town.

59 South Quay, seen here in 1925, was known as Pagets House for Samuel Paget lived here, father of the great Victorian surgeon Sir James Paget. To the north of the house is Row 139, Paget's Row. In 1863 this became the School of Art, Navigation and Science, an establishment which provided both day and evening classes for male and female students. It later became the Borough of Great Yarmouth Municipal School of Science, teaching subjects such as building and machine construction, chemistry and mathematics.

The art class at the School of Art. Note the formal wear with the tail coat worn by one of the students. The art department moved to a new purpose built Art School in Trafalgar Road in the 1930's leaving 59 South Quay as the School of Science until the building was destroyed in the Second World War.

The Rows Today

A walk around the old town today will reveal many interesting traces of the medieval Row system. The entrances to many Rows can be found along Northgate Street, the Market Place, King Street and part of South Quay although unfortunately not a single complete medieval Row has survived the ravages of war and subsequent rebuilding. Of the 145 Rows which existed and were numbered in the 19th century small sections of over half are still to be found today. The numbers are painted in white on black panels at the ends of the surviving Rows and in recent years many name plates have been erected by the local Archaeological Society. In the Market Place Row 46, beside the card shop, is possibly the best example of how a Row of the 19th century appeared, narrow, curved and with the buildings at the entrance joining above the Row. It has already been mentioned how many Rows have disappeared in the last fifty years as rebuilding has swallowed them up, a practice that is now more controlled as the whole area of the Rows is covered by conservation orders.

In King Street, between Rows 89 and 90 stands the only surviving timber framed jettied building in the town, now a Chinese Restaurant. At one time there were many houses of this type in the Rows. Other medieval Row buildings to be seen today include the Merchants House and Row 111 houses, preserved by English Heritage. In these two buildings can be seen a large collection of doors, fireplaces, cupboards, woodwork and other artefacts rescued from Row houses during the demolition years of the early 1950's. Many of the doors have intricately painted panels and glass, no doubt efforts by the inhabitants to brighten up what was often a gloomy interior. Moulded ceilings and panelled walls give an interesting insight into what the interior of many of the larger Row houses were like before they were divided into smaller units.

To the rear of the Old White Lion public house in Nottingham Way, are two shops which were originally in Row 130, the only Row other than Market and Broad Row where shops were to be found. Troll carts posed a problem for the inhabitants of many Rows and wooden 'fenders' were fixed to walls to prevent damage. One such protective device can still be seen in Row 83, fixed to the wall of the building which is now the museum. Although much restored there is still some original timber to be seen. Iron posts were placed against walls at the corners of many Rows for the same reason and one of these is still to be seen in King Street, on the corner of Row 116.

Today there are still traces of medieval Yarmouth to be found in what remains of the Rows, several examples of early doorways, windows and walls are visible to the keen observer.

Seventeenth century houses in Row 118 before demolition. These houses were surveyed in 1943 and were typical Row houses with a single room on each floor, an attic and a cellar. Much of the original 17th century building still survived.

The Old White Lion in King Street c1930 with Row 130 and Leach & Sons ironmongers on the right, now Nottingham Way.

The Streets of the Old Town

The Quays

North Quay extends from the medieval North West Tower to Hall Quay and has a frontage onto two stretches of water, at the northern end the river Bure, or North river, and at its southern end Breydon Water. In the 17th century this part of the town was known as the North End and was so little frequented that the houses on the quay were described as "abutting upon a meadow next the river". The northern part of the quay was frequented by the Broads wherries and here cargoes brought from the Broadland area such as bricks were unloaded before being carted into the town. Many wherrymen lived in the Rows leading off this part of the quay and when St Andrews church was built in 1859 it was described as the wherrymens church.

A bridge was first erected over the North river in 1829, a suspension bridge which replaced a ferry. In 1845 this bridge collapsed with the loss of 79 lives and was replaced two years later with a bridge that was to last until 1952. The present bridge was opened in 1972 and is the fourth on the site. In 1848 the railway built a bridge further south which necessitated the demolition of Pagets Brewery. This bridge was to carry the rail line onto the quay and southwards to the other end of the town. The bridge was rebuilt in 1887 and today is a foot bridge to the railway station and the Asda Supermarket.

The first building to be erected on the open land fronting Breydon Water was a post mill built by Christopher Short in 1579 and known as the Quay Mill (see Row 34). At the southern end of this part of the quay was a building known as the Norwich Warehouse and from here wherries provided a daily service to and from Norwich.

North Quay leads into Hall Quay, an area where the buildings have always been set back from the riverside and which in the 15th century was the most fashionable part of the town. This was known as the Foreland before the first Town Hall was built at the southern end in 1716. In the 19th century it was also referred to as the Short Quay. This has always been the main crossing point to the west bank of the river, the first bridge being built in 1427 to replace a ferry. There have been seven bridges across the river at this point, the present Haven Bridge being opened in 1930.

Hall Quay leads to South Quay which extends from the Town Hall (opened in 1882) to the site of the medieval South Gate (demolished 1812) from where the road becomes Southgate Road. An increase in trade and commerce in the 16th century led to the formation of a quay along this section of the river and it was not long before the open land fronting the quay was lined with

Custom House Quay. The arched entrance to Row 103 can be seen beside the Custom House and further to the right is the Town House (see Row 106). The jib of the Town Crane, demolished in 1983, can be seen on the far right.

This view of South Quay dates from c1872 and shows the Ship Chandlers shop of S J Fill at number 41. This business later became the Gt Yarmouth Steam Tug Company which finished in 1939. The last tug owned by this company was the United Services.

The lamp post is outside the Fishery public house which in 1802 had changed its name to the Newcastle Tavern and later the Ferry Hotel. This closed in 1941 and today is the corner of Nottingham Way.

imposing merchants houses, many still existing at the northern end of the quay. In the 18th century Defoe, speaking of the Yarmouth Quay said, "in this pleasant and agreeable range of houses are some magnificent buildings, merchants' houses which look like little palaces rather than the dwelling houses of private men". He also described the quay as, "the finest, largest and longest in Europe except that of Seville in Spain". Sylas Neville considered it, "one of the noblest in the world". In the early 19th century a double row of trees was planted along the quay forming a promenade from the Town Hall to Friars Lane. In 1999 this part of the quay side was once again planted with trees.

George Street

The most westerly of the three narrow north-south streets which ran through the old town. This originally led from Fullers Hill to Furlong End, another name for Hall Quay. In 1291 it was known as Northgate. Today little remains of the original George Street where in 1886 there were thirteen public houses. Only at the southern end near Broad Row have the old buildings survived. At the northern end many buildings were taken into the Brewery in 1890. Fullers Passage was a continuation of George Street from the north side of Fullers Hill to White Horse Plain and Northgate Street. At one time this was the main route into the town from the North Gate to the Hall Quay.

Middlegate Street

The original Middlegate Street, documented from 1250, began from Hall Plain and continued southwards until it reached Friars Lane (at one time known as South Street). For many years it was known as Gaol Street because the Tolhouse, between Rows 106 and 108, housed the town gaol from 1552 until 1875. The Corporation changed the name of the street back to Middlegate in 1870. Today almost nothing remains of the original narrow street, the bombing of the Second World War and subsequent redevelopment removing nearly all traces. The only buildings remaining are the Tolhouse and the buildings to the south of it and the Ship public house and the adjoining buildings. The old Middlegate Street was a continuous line of houses, small shops, public houses and other commercial premises with thirty Rows leading east into Howard Street and twenty-six Rows leading west to South Quay. In 1880 a new Police and Fire Station was built near the Town Hall in Middlegate Street. At this time the town constabulary consisted of a chief constable and 57 men.

A troll cart outside the Tolhouse in Middlegate Street late in the 19th century. By this time the narrow troll cart was being replaced by larger vehicles, those left being used mainly for delivering beer (which this one appears to be doing) or in the fishing industry.

Below is the shop of Roland Tropman at 125 and 126 Middlegate Street about 1930. This shop was on the west side of the street, next to Row 136. Mrs Tropman is standing in the doorway

Howard Street

This is one of the oldest streets in the town. In its original form it ran from the south west corner of Church Plain southwards to finish in a dead end at Row 90. The northern end of the street as far as Broad Row was, from 1351, known as Middle Street, the continuation from Broad Row being known as Blind Middle Street. The northern end was also known as Wrestlers Street and in the late 18th century renamed Charlotte Street after the popular daughter of George IV. In 1882 the southern end was renamed Howard Street in honour of the Norfolk family of that name. Today it is known as Howard Street North and South, the division still being at Broad Row although there is not much left of Howard Street south of Regent Street. The oldest building today in Howard Street is the Friends Meeting House, parts of which date from the early 14th century when it was a cell of the Augustinian Priory at Gorleston. From 1694 it has been used by the Quakers and the building was reconstructed in 1807 into its present form. The burial ground at the rear has not been used for some years.

Howard Street had the distinction of being the town's first one-way street. In 1930 it was made one-way from Regent Street to Church Plain between the hours of 8am and 7.30pm, except Sundays. In 1935 it was made permanently one-way but today only small sections of Howard Street have this restriction.

King Street

For many years one of the principal streets in the town this runs from the south west corner of the Market Place in a southerly direction the length of the old town to Friars Lane. The name is in commemoration of the visit to the town by King Charles II in September 1671 when he was, "infinitely pleased with the town and port; he had not thought he had such a place in his dominions". This was an abrupt about turn by a Corporation that had been staunchly anti-royalist throughout the years of the Civil War.

Until 1678 the eastern side of King Street was open land to the town wall, known as the Deneside. This open area was originally part of the towns defences and was later used for ropewalks by the many rope makers in the town. Demand for extra building space led to the Corporation selling this land and soon many large buildings, separated by short Rows, were erected here (see Row 64). After the building of St Georges Chapel in 1715 this part of the street was known for several years as Chapel Street.

On the corner of Row 72 in Hall Plain was the restaurant of Walter Grimes here advertising Bed & Breakfast for 2/6 ($12^1/_2$p) in 1910. This later became the office of the Yarmouth Mercury before it moved to Regent Street. On the right is Camplings the printers which later became the Yare Printing Company.

Regent Street

Until the early years of the 19th century the only east-west route across the old town, apart from the narrow Rows, was either Fuller's Hill in the north or Friars Lane in the south. This caused great inconvenience particularly when it was necessary to move large loads from the Quayside to the Market Place. The solution to this was to construct a new road across the town and a site was chosen to the north of the Town Hall. Rows 68 and 69 taken into the new street which cut across Howard Street (then Blind Middle Street) to terminate in King Street. On 29 September 1813 the mayor opened the new street and officially named it Regent Street. It had cost the town £30,000 and was at first a street of private houses, described in 1819 as, "being replete with genteel houses and private lodgings on either side". Several of these private houses soon became offices and eventually shops were established.

The Troll Cart

First introduced in the late 15th century and then known as the Harry-Carry this vehicle was designed to negotiate the narrow Rows and convey goods to all parts of the town. The Yarmouth Cart as it was later called was about three feet six inches wide and up to twelve feet in length with two small wheels under the body of the cart. In many cases the wheels were solid wood with no tyres. The cart was drawn by one horse, the driver standing on the cart when empty or walking by the side when it was loaded. Another version of this vehicle was known as the Yarmouth Coach, designed to carry two people and used mainly during the bathing season to carry visitors from the town to the seaside. These vehicles were usually painted red, blue or green and Defoe described them as, "wheelbarrows drawn by one horse, without any covering" and another writer said, "they are the most whimsical carriages in the kingdom".

After the opening of Regent Street the need for the narrow carts declined as they could be replaced by larger vehicles. By the turn of the 20th century they had almost disappeared completely until in 1902 Arthur Patterson obtained what was claimed to be the last example of this unique form of transport, then in the ownership of Lacons Brewery, and presented it to the Tolhouse museum. Unfortunately this was destroyed by fire during the Second World War and the example to be seen there today is a replica. Another replica was made more recently, in 1996 by the Yceni Workshop in Artillery Square. This is now displayed, as part of a floral arrangement, at the southern end of the Market Place.

Row 142 photographed in June 1939 looking towards South Quay. A coal truck can be seen on the quayside tramway in this, one of the last photographs to be taken of the Rows before the war commenced only three months later. The end of the town's medieval street layout was now only a few months away.

Row Names

Absolon's	Row 37
Adams the Baker's	132
Aldred's	74/83
Almshouse	54/136
Ames the Antiquary's	88
Ames the Shoemaker's	36
Andrew's	103
Ange	144
Anthony Taylor's	108
Arbon the Painter's	85
Arnold the Brewer's	102
Ballast Keel	Row 117
Balls and Pownall Fruiterer's	90
Bank Paved	53
Baptist Meeting	14
Baptist Meeting North	82
Baptist Meeting South	85
Barber the Stationer's	55
Barker's North	73
Barker's South	74
Barnaby the Baker's	30
Barnby the Liquor Merchant's	42
Barnes	97
Barnes the Grocer's	22
Barett's	20
Barthlemew's	48
Bassingthwaite the Baker's	60
Batchelor's	115
Bateman's	64
Baxfield's	23
Bayly's Surgeon	97
Beckett's	131
Bee Hive	26
Bellamy's	90
Bellamy the Butcher's	110
Bellamy the Baker's	133
Bell's	97
Benett the Cooper's	102
Ben Dowson's	62
Bessey's	9
Bessey's Half	9
Bethabara	92

Bett's	Row 78
Bird in Hand	2
Black Horse	2
Blake the Linen Draper's	49
Black Swan	51
Blanchflower's Half	135$\frac{1}{2}$
Blick's	97
Blower the Cabinet Maker's	39
Blue Anchor	24
Blue Bell	118
Boatswains Call	73
Body Snatcher's	6
Bond's	128
Bond the Druggist's	63
Boulter the Baker's	3
Bracey's	136
Bradnack's	119
Bream's	68
Brett's North	14
Brett's South	15
Brewery	19
British Lion Alley	51$\frac{1}{2}$
Browne's	6
Brown the Candlemaker's	10
Brown the Grocer's	78
Brown the Maltster's	112
Buck	52/97
Bumpstead's	22
Bunting's	52
Burman's	5
Bush Tavern	96
Butcher's	135
Calver's	Row 126
Cambridge	78
Carter's	83
Captain Christmas's	121
Carpenter's Arms	57
Carrington's	92
Cart & Horse	137
Castle	99
Cat & Monkey	124
Chambers the Sailmaker's	112
Chapel	103/105
Chapel Paved	107

Chapman's	Row 5
Charles Moore's	38
Charles Palmer's	83
Charles Symond's	101
Child the Blacksmith's	141
Church's	62
Cloister	91½
Clowe's	55
Coach & Horses	25/77
Coalmeter's	61
Cobb's	25
Cobb the Curier's South	27
Cobb's North	73
Cobb's South	74
Cobb the Printer's	55
Cock Half	135½
Colby's North	123
Colby's South	124
Common Ramp	1
Conge	28
Cook Ellis's	132
Cooper's	83
Cory's	76
Costerton's	100
Costerton the Surgeon's	52
Couldham's	119/106
Craske the Baker's	70
Creed's	88
Crisp the Carter's	133
Crome's	81
Crown & Anchor	59
Crown & Heart	85
Cubitt the Painter's	71
Cup's	65
Custom House	103
Custom House South	104
Daking the Brazier's	Row 65
Dassett's	43
Davy the Watchmaker's	29
Dawson's	119
Delf's	132
Dendy's	66
Dene Side Austin	60
Dene Well	140

Dog & Duck	Row 138
Doughty's	3
Doughty the Grocer's	105
Doughty the Leathercutter's	25/27
Doughty's North	25
Doughty's South	27
Douglas's	6
Dove	119
Dover Colby's North Wall	123
Dover Colby's South Wall	124
Dover Court	132
Draper the Butcher's	95
Dr Borrett's	109
Dr Collier's	104
Dr Costerton's	52
Dr Farmington's	33
Dr Meadow's	109
Dr Penrice's	105
Dr Smith's	26
Drum	120
Druid	129
Duncan's Head	120
Dutch Chapel	106
Eagle Half	Row 34½
Earl St Vincent	140
East & West Flegg	2
Ecclestone the Grocer's	4
Edinburgh	29
Elephant & Castle	58
Ellis the Brushmaker	38
Emm's	135
England's	108
Erchard's	134
Errington's	113
Excise Office	56
Factory	Row 128
Fassett's	74
Felstead's	142
Feltham's	22
Ferrier's	38
Ferrier the Surgeon's	113
Ferry Boat	8
Fielding's	86

Fighting Cock	Row 25	Gurney's Bank	Row 55
Fill the Auctioneer's	21	Half	Row 51½
Fisher's	86	Half Moon	29
Fishing Boat	142	Half Moon North	26
Foreman the Baker's	70	Half Moon South	29
Fourteen Stars	145	Half Moon Tap	26
Foulsham's	24	Hall the Blacksmith's	118
Foundry	127	Hans Herring	89
Fowler the Grocer's	88	Harboard the Pastrycook's	80
Free Library	108	Hardware's	80
Freemason's Arms	35	Harman's	35
Freeman and May's	10	Harmer's	80
Friends	129	Harrison's	90
Friendly Society	104	Hastings the Pawnbroker's	116
Fromow the Barber's	23	Hat & Feather	145
Fulcher the Grocer's	40	Hayes the Butcher's	135
Fulcher the Pawnbroker's	123	Haynes the Peruke Maker's	72
Fuller's	96	Herring's	89
Fuller's South	100	Hogarth's	43
		Holmes South	112
Gallon Can	Row 117	Homfray's	62
Gaol North	106	Horn	10
Gaol Paved	108	Horse & Cart	137
Garden	13/36	Houghton the Baker's	141
Garwood the Glazier's	128	Huke's	121
G D Palmer's	137	Huke the Carpenter's	121
George	117	Humber Keel	120
George IV	87	Hunt the Glazier's	42
George & Dragon	12	Hurry's	69/92
Girling's	66		
Glass House	37	Ives the Antiquary's	Row 140
Globe	35	James Burton's Half	Row 64
Goddard the Whitesmith's	93	Jays Chemist's	65
Golden Ball	47	J C Smith's	86
Golden Keys	7	J D Palmer's	83
Golden Lion	25	Jeffery's	15
Good the Grocer's	126	Jews	42
Goymer's Meeting North	14	J F Costerton's	100
Goymer's Meeting South	15	John Berney's	81
Graves the Pieman's	133	John Cooper's South	136
Gregory Harrison's	129	John Cooper's North	133
Greyfriars	91½	John Fisher's	108/123
Grief's	137	John Ireland's	84
Grosse's	143		
Gun	125		

John Taylor's	Row129	Mayer's	Row 144
Jolly Maltsters	79	Mayor Ramey's	67
Jone's	144	Meall's	55
Joseph Cotman's	94	Meggy's	55
Josh Peartree's	117	Mew's	64
		Mew's Half	90
Kemps	126	Meyrick's	81
Kerrison's Coffee Tavern	142	Miller the Basketmaker's	73
Kings Head	32/93	Mission to Seamen	139
Kings Head North	29	Miss Paterson's	80
Kings Head South	32	Mitchells School	59
Kingston House	Broad Row	Money Office	87
King the Baker's	41/93	Moon the Cabinet Maker's	43
Kittywitches	95	Moore the Blacksmith's	72
Knights the Baker's	134	Morling the Grocer's	143
		Mouse the Pawnbroker's	36
Lacon's	Row 13/16	Mr Brightwen's	57
Lacon's Brewery	16		
Lacon's Office	19	Nags Head	Row 46/145
Lamb	51	Nall's	63
Lane the Taylor's	50	Nathaniel Fish's	115
Last the Baker's	58	Neal the Shoemaker's	36
Laws & Lamb the Butcher's	124	Neave's	144
Lawyer Bell's	97	Nelson Tavern	141
Lee the Pawnbroker's	133	Newcastle Tavern	129
Lettis's	81	New Fountain	136
Lieutenant White's	114	New Prison	110
Lion & Lamb	109	New White Lion	134
Liverpool Tavern	140	Nicholas Cutting's	67
Lobster	79	Nightingale the Confectioner's	97
Lone the Pawnbroker's	80	Nightingale the Barber's	33
Lorimer the Grocer's	26	Nine Parish	31
Lucas's	111	Norfolk Hero	97
Luson's	111	Norfolk Tavern	77
		Normans	26
Mack the Tinsmith's	Row 125	Norman the Cabinet Maker's	39
Male the Chemist's	70	North	10
Mariners	65	North Custom House	103
Mariners Compass	142	North Garden	11
Markland's	44	Nottingham Arms	145
Marsh's	85/132		
Martin's	104		
Martin the Shoemaker's	122	Old Fountain	Row 77
Matthew Ward's	117	Old Fountain North	75
Matthew's the Bakers	139	Old Fountain Tap	77
Maye the Baker's	143	Old Hannah's	90

A troll cart in the Market Place in 1870. This vehicle, unique to Yarmouth was designed to travel through the narrow Rows. Replicas can be seen today in the Tolhouse museum and in the Market Place.

Old Hannah's Back	Row 89	Perry the Oatmeal Maker's	Row 110
Old Library	85	Pickard's	24
Old Meeting House	92	Pigeon	140/142
Old Meeting South	96	Pipemaker's	47
Old Post House	107	Pleasants the Butcher's	132
Old Post Office	63	Pleasants the Grocer's	143
Old Prison	135	Plumer's	116
Old White Lion	130	Plumer's School	116
Orfeur's	132	Popinjay	61
Ostend Market	60	Poppy's	75
Ostend West	61	Post House	107
Oxford	60	Post Office	63
		Post Office Half	$63\frac{1}{2}$
Packet Office	Row 102	Pot in Hand North	78
Paget's	139	Pot in Hand South	79
Page the Pipemaker's	47	Prichard's	64
Palgrave's	106	Prison	110
Palmers Arcade	54		
Peacock	74/142	Quaker's	Row 63
Peer's	76	Quay Angel	123
Penrice Back	94	Quay Austin	61
Penrice Stables	101	Quay Mill	34
Penny's	26	Quay Mill Alley	$34\frac{1}{2}$

Queens Head North	Row 29	Sons of Commerce	Row 100
Queens Head South	32	South Garden	13
		Southgate the Butcher's	144
Rackhams	Row 6	Sowell the Painter's	100
Ramp	1	Spanton's	128
Rampart	1	Spilling's	75
Randall's	60	Split Gutter	5
Red House	58	Spooner's	100
Red Lion	109	Spotted Cow	141
Rev Cooper's	105	Spratt the Shoemaker's	133
Rev Green's Meeting	14/15	Spread Eagle	122
Rev Welham's	69	Star & Garter	57
Reynold's	101	Starling the Hatter's	78
Richmond the Cabinet Maker's	50	Star Tavern	67
Rivett the Baker's	93	Stamp Office	66
Robert Warmington's	104	Step Paved	107
Robin's Half	126	Stevenson's	140
Robinson the Grocer's	119	Steward's	87/111
Rolling the Baker's	4	Steward the Chemist's	20
Rose & Crown	41/137	St Georges East	107
Rowe's	35	St Georges Paved West	108
Royal Exchange	103	St Johns Head	45
Rumble the China Dealer's	81	St Peters	130
		St Peters East	130
		St Peters Half Alley	126
Saffrey the Brewer's	Row 103	St Peters Paved West	129
Sam Hurry's	116	Swan	20
Samuel Palmer's	61	Swannard's	104
Samuel Tolver's	76	Swinden the Historian's	82
Sarah Martin's	57	Symond's	62/71
Saving Bank	56/66	Symonds the Hairdresser's	50
Sayer the Attorney's	83	Synagogue	42
Says Corner North	17		
Says Corner South	18	Taylor's	Row 108
Scott the Baker's	127	Taylor and Fulcher North	40
Sewell the Grocer's	46	Taylor and Fulcher South	43
Ship Tavern	84	Taylor the Surgeon's	26
Shuckforth the Basketmaker's	22	Thaxter's	142
Singen's	45	Thomas Hurry's	116
Sir E Travers	111	Thomas Lucas's	68
Sir Sidney Smith's	85	Thompson's	127
Skill's	55	Thorndick's	144
Sloman's	63	Thornton's	4
Smith the Baker's	54	Thornton the Grocer's	4
Smith the Cabinet Maker's	21	Three Cranes	106
Snatchbody	6		

Alleys and Passages

Acknowledgments

Once again many people have helped and contributed towards the information that has been included in this book. Most of the photographs come from my own collection but I would like to thank Peter Allard and John Taylor for additional photographs from their collections. Alec McEwen kindly read and commented on my original draft and Paul Rutledge allowed me to use material from his research on the early history of the town, previously published in Yarmouth Archaeology, for which I am very grateful. The final choice of photographs was a difficult task and I thank my wife Jan for her patience and help with this. As in previous books I have made every effort to establish copyright for the images used but in some cases this has been impossible as the true origin of some photographs is obscure. Anyone with a copyright claim is asked to contact the publisher in writing.

Further Reading

The Perlustration of Gt Yarmouth. 3 Vols. by C J Palmer. 1875

Origins and Early Development of Gt Yarmouth by P Rutledge. Yarmouth Archaeology 1990 and 1999.

Report of the General Health Board by W Lea. 1850

Some 17th C. Houses in Gt Yarmouth by St J O'Neil. 1953

English Place Names Society. Vol 72. 1996

SPAB survey of Gt Yarmouth Rows. 1936. Unpublished.

The Rows of Gt Yarmouth. 6 Parts by M Teun. 1987-1991

The Rows of Gt Yarmouth by C Tooke. 1987.